THE FULL STORY

The Official Photographic
and Statistical Review of
Rugby World Cup 1999

PUBLISHERS

Managing Editor: Bill Cotton

Programme Publications Ltd.

39a East Street,

Epsom, Surrey, KT17 1BL

Telephone: 01372 743377

Fax: 01372 743399

email: lynn@programmepubs.demon.co.uk

www.eventprogrammes.com

DESIGN

Design Consultant: Nick Kelly

Design and Artwork:

David Kelly, Emma Robinson

Creative Services (1998) Ltd.

Century Building, 20 Tower Street,

Liverpool, L3 4BJ

Telephone: 0151 707 4200

Fax: 0151 707 4201

ISDN: 0151 702 8660

email: dave@creativesl.demon.co.uk

PHOTOGRAPHS

Allsport UK Ltd

3 Greenlea Park, Prince George's Road,

London, SW19 2JD

Telephone: 0181 685 1010

Fax: 0181 648 5240

www.allsport.com

REPRO & PRINT

Hyway Printing Group

Mulberry Business Centre,

Quebec Way, Surrey Quays,

London, SE16 1LB

Telephone: 0171 232 5000

Fax: 0171 232 5104

ISDN: 0171 232 5117

www.hyway.co.uk

BINDING

Hunter & Foulis Ltd.

Bridgeside, McDonald Road.

Edinburgh, EH7 4NP

Telephone: 0131 556 7947

Fax: 0131 557 3911

Email: mail@hunterfoulis.com.uk

The Official Photographic and Statistical Review of Rugby World Cup 1999

PROGRAMME
PUBLICATIONS

Programme Publications
39a East Street, Epsom, Surrey KT17 1BL

Published 1999

ISBN: 0 9531528-8-X

Designed by Creative Services (1998) Ltd.

Printed in the UK by Hyway Printing Group Ltd.

Bound in the UK by Hunter Foulis Ltd.

Contents

Foreword by Leo Williams, Chairman, Rugby World Cup Ltd.

It is a pleasure to be able to write a foreword for a book that brings together glimpses of a great sporting event. Immortalised by AllSport photographers, RWC'99 will remain in memory as the greatest rugby event of the century and the most successful RWC to date. This book will provide both the rugby expert and the armchair supporter with a compendium of the most exciting moments of the 41-match marathon. These images demonstrate the game's appeal, its ability to both enchant and electrify.

As predicted, this Tournament surpassed all records of participants, spectators, media coverage and moments of rugby excellence. Young stars have emerged on the world scene, nations new to RWC, like Uruguay and Spain, demonstrated their considerable potential. The commercial revenue generated by the competition will underpin the development of the game worldwide for years to come. The rugby was magnificent. The spectators, and the knowledgeable and generous crowds of Cardiff and Twickenham in particular, were marvellous. The worldwide media coverage was sensational. I personally enjoyed the match between Romania and the USA as much as I enjoyed the two semi-finals, a sample of the splendidly contrasting styles this great game generates.

Stade de France and Twickenham sold out for matches involving teams other than France and England respectively, not to mention a crowd of over 60,000 watching the 3rd and 4th place play-off at the Millennium Stadium. More than 30,000 spectators saw Ireland v Argentina in Lens, a soccer strong-hold in the North of France. These are powerful statements about the drawing power and the success of the Tournament, which at its fourth birthday, has matured into a superb competition.

But this magnificent Tournament was only the last phase of a worldwide story. Spare a thought for the 65 nations involved over three years in 133 qualifying matches played all over the world from Raratonga to Tbilisi, and Krasnoyarsk to Casablanca.

The superb standards set in the third RWC in South Africa in 1995 have been surpassed by the fourth Tournament. RWC now ranks among the top four sporting events in the world in terms of popularity, public appeal, and commercial potential. The 1999 Tournament will be regarded in retrospect as a watershed in rugby's global expansion.

Leo Williams
Chairman, RWC Ltd.

iRB INTERNATIONAL RUGBY BOARD A message from Vernon Pugh QC, Chairman, International Rugby Board

Another Rugby World Cup, the fourth staged under the auspices of the IRB since 1987, is now history but the memories linger on.

Any tournament of this nature, drawing on the talents of 20 teams of varying abilities, will have its highs and lows, glorious passages of play to confirm rugby's worth as a superb athletic spectacle and nail-biting finishes to many of the matches.

On balance, I believe RWC '99 achieved all its main objectives. It drew record crowds and television audiences along the way to producing a worthy champion in Australia who, in 2003, become the first country to actually host a defence of the William Webb Ellis Cup.

France, the beaten finalists, did sensationally well in their semi-final triumph over New Zealand and added enjoyment to the tournament.

The defending champions, South Africa, eventually finished third after being edged out by Australia for a place in the Millennium Stadium Final after a game overflowing with tension and courage while the fourth-placed All Blacks had no answer to French brilliance of the highest possible order in the second semi-final.

We also admired the manner in which Argentina overcame pre-tournament uncertainties, how Fiji at last showed they can combine innate flair with a focused forward effort and how bravely all the teams in the lower finishing order stayed on task no matter how stiff the challenge.

RWC '99 was the very first Rugby World Cup since professionalism was introduced in 1995. The pace and power of the game has altered and reflects the advent of full-time rugby for many of the top teams.

However, predictions that the gap between professionals and amateurs would be reflected in huge scores simply did not materialise. Instead, we had five weeks in which to appreciate the sport's unique qualities, the outstanding skills and intense physicality, the scope for genius as well as raw power, and the genuine respect and sportsmanship of the participants towards each other.

We could have asked for nothing more.

Vernon Pugh QC
Chairman, International Rugby Board

Allsport Rugby World Cup Photographers Team

Alex Livesey

Ben Radford

Clive Mason

Gary Prior

Michael Steele

Mike Hewitt

Phil Cole

David Rogers

Shaun Botterill

Stu Forster

Images telling the story of each encounter, plus training, press conferences and features went out electronically 'Live' every day to the world-wide Allsport network of media contacts plus Allsport offices and agents in 42 countries.

Allsport has delivered the very best in action photography from rugby's flagship event to its millions of fans around the world.

ALLSPORT RUGBY WORLD CUP TEAM

Photographers: David Rogers, Mike Hewitt, Ross Kinnaird, Shaun Botterill, Stu Forster, Ben Radford, Clive Mason, Gary M Prior, Michael Steele, Phil Cole, Alex Livesey
Managing Editor: Steve Rose
Rugby Editor: Justin Davies

DAVID ROGERS

Allsport's Chief Rugby Photographer joined the company in 1993 and is now a familiar face on the circuit. 'D.R.' has covered all four Rugby World Cups as well as five British Lions tours, countless Five Nations, Tri Nations and Super 12 championships plus league and cup rugby in the UK and around the world. He has received numerous photographic awards for his work over the years, including RFU Photographer of the Year.

Allsport's involvement with Rugby World Cup 1999 began long before the Opening Ceremony in Cardiff on 1st October 1999.

Our photographers travelled the world covering decisive games at the qualification stage. Allsport was in Buenos Aires to record the historic moment when Uruguay reached the finals for the very first time. We witnessed similar scenes of joy from qualifying matches as far afield as Georgia, Morocco, Singapore, China and Australasia.

Prior to the first game, a team of dedicated Allsport staff was put in place to ensure in-depth coverage of the event. A minimum of two photographers and one technician attended every game to capture every ruck, maul, tackle and try. Up to four photographers covered key games, and six Allsport photographers were at the Final - more than any other photographic agency in the world.

The Captains and
The Kings depart...

As Rugby World Cup 99 begins to settle
into legend, the discussions, the
arguments, the opinions begin. The
triumphs and disasters are endlessly
re-evaluated. Opinions begin to
marinate in the collective memory.
The greats of the game become
immortalised, the lesser talents
illuminated by their glancing moments
of fame.

The vivid colliding memories of
collective courage and heart stopping
flashes of solo brilliance are the essence
of Rugby World Cup 1999. This is the
full story.

The Date: 1st October 1999

The Place: The Millennium Stadium, Cardiff,

The Occasion: Opening Ceremony, Rugby World Cup 99

Prince Charles declares the tournament open

Bryn Terfel and Shirley Bassey

Cerys Matthews of Catatonia

Gwyn Jones, former Welsh captain, with the trophy

Opening match of RWC99: Argentina kick off against Wales

THE 1999 RUGBY WORLD CUP

POOL A

South Africa

Scotland

Spain

Uruguay

South Africa maintained their 100 per cent World Cup record and now stand on played nine, won nine on the world stage after topping their Scotland-based group.

While the Springboks go straight into a quarter-final showdown in Paris with the winners of the England v Fiji play-off, the Scots have to negotiate the play-off hurdle of facing Samoa at Murrayfield and with that a showdown with tournament favourites New Zealand in Edinburgh.

The 'Boks opened their defence of the Webb Ellis trophy by beating reigning Five Nations champions Scotland 46-29 in front of a 62,000 crowd at Murrayfield.

In what was always going to be the crunch match of the group the Springboks ran in six tries - including a rumbling effort from prop Ollie le Roux after he was found lurking out in the midfield.

The Scots drew first blood with the first of wing Kenny Logan's four penalty goals after just nine minutes and they held the lead four times before the 'Boks finished with a flourish.

Flanker Martin Leslie profited from a series of punishing drives into South African territory and centre Alan Tait crossed the South African line five minutes from the end.

However, any flickering faint home hopes were extinguished as André Venter and Joost van der Westhuizen

Scotland v South Africa: Joost van der Westhuizen, South Africa's captain, launches his backs.

pounced for tries in the dying minutes, fly half Jannie de Beer ending up with 14 points.

The previous day Uruguay had launched their debut appearance by beating Spain 27-15 in Galashiels, as they outscored the Spaniards 4-0 in tries.

There was more woe for Spain when they went down 47-3 to South Africa in the second round - but they won a host of new friends for their never-say-die defensive display.

The 'Boks did manage seven tries, but for them there was never the ruthless cutting edge to turn it into a rout as the Spaniards gave everything in a sterling performance.

Uruguay also bowed out in defiant mood, holding the world champions to a 39-3 winning margin and ending their first venture in the tournament in third place. On top of failing to impress, the Springboks had centre Brendan Venter sent off for stamping.

On the credit side, South African captain van der Westhuizen extended his national try scoring record to the 27 mark with one of their five tries, replacement Albert van den Berg snatching a brace near the end as the South Americans tired.

Although the Murrayfield crowd failed to make it into five figures, Scotland notched up their first win with a 43-12 romp against Uruguay.

There were six tries for the Scots -

Martin Leslie crossing for the second World Cup match in a row - with Logan adding another 13 points to his personal tally with five conversions and a penalty.

With the top spot having been as good as settled in the first round, it was left up to the Scots to finish the group stage with a routine 48-0 win over Spain.

New Zealand-born Cameron Mather made a superb debut, collecting two of the seven Scottish tries, and although the Spaniards battled to the end they were left empty-handed and on their way home.

Scotland v Uruguay: Scotland's Gordon Simpson scores

Across page:
Top left: Scotland v Uruguay
Hanging onto the shirt tail

Bottom left: Scotland v Spain
Duncan Hodge of Scotland skips through for a try

Main picture: South Africa v Uruguay
Robbie Fleck of South Africa on the burst

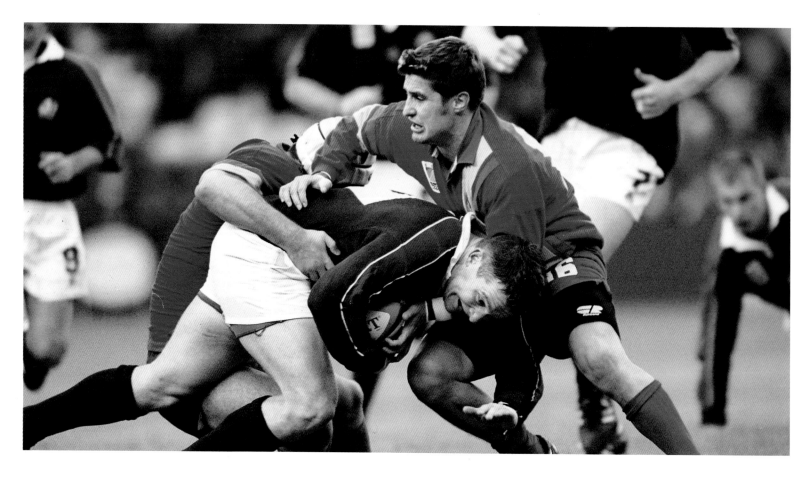

Top: Scotland v Spain
James McLaren is wrapped up by a determined
Spanish defence

Right: South Africa v Uruguay
Albert van den Berg (South Africa)
stopped in his tracks

THE 1999 RUGBY WORLD CUP

POOL B

New Zealand

England

Italy

Tonga

New Zealand v Tonga: Jeff Wilson (New Zealand) kicks ahead

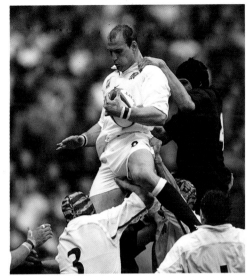

England v New Zealand:
England's Lawrence Dallaglio takes a lineout

New Zealand confirmed their status as tournament favourites by finishing clear at the top of the group with nine points and condemning runners-up England to an extra fixture against Fiji at Twickenham in the play-offs.

The All Blacks shrugged off their recent poor record at Twickenham to win the big showdown with Martin Johnson's team 30-16 in a pulsating collision of giants.

But the Kiwis had opened in far more subdued manner in the less celebrated rugby surrounds of Ashton Gate, Tonga relishing their first international against their relatively near neighbours by giving every bit as good as they got.

A final flurry of 26 points in the final quarter gave the All Blacks a 45-9 victory but they certainly knew they had been in a game though Jonah Lomu announced he is going to be a main man again by pounding over for two of the five tries.

England made light of their Italian job as Italy were blown away 67-7 as England raced to their new record mark in a World Cup finals match.

Fly half Jonny Wilkinson enjoyed a field day, rattling up a new individual match record for his country with a 32-point haul made up of a try, six conversions and five penalty goals.

But the real business took place in front of a capacity Twickenham crowd and this time it was the All Blacks who struck the big psychological blow.

In a match of huge intensity, pace and skill, the crowd were treated to a marvellous contest that stood at 16-16 before tries from that man mountain, 6 feet 5 inches Lomu, and Byron Kelleher settled matters.

Jeff Wilson had scored the first New Zealand try after 18 minutes and although centre Phil de Glanville crossed for England half an hour later and Wilkinson weighed in with another 11 points, the All Blacks were the ones on the fast track to the quarter-finals.

There was also plenty of thrills and excitement when Tonga snatched a dramatic 28-25 victory over Italy under the Welford Road lights, Tongan full back Sateki Tu'ipulotu the man-of-the-moment with a match winning drop goal at the death.

If Italy went close on that occasion,

there was nothing but despair for the Azzurri when the All Blacks showed no mercy in romping to a 101-3 victory at Huddersfield.

It was one-way traffic after a spirited

New Zealand v Italy: Jonah Lomu lends a helping hand

Italian opening, the floodgates opening and the individual records flowing. Jeff Wilson became his country's leading try scorer as he swept past John Kirwan's 35-try mark with a hat-trick and fellow wing Lomu became the top try scorer in World Cup history with 12, one more than England's Rory Underwood.

New Zealand rattled up 14 tries with fly half Tony Brown taking the chance to make his mark with 38 points, made up of a try, three penalty goals and 12 conversions.

Determined to prove that anything the All Blacks could do, England could too, Johnson's men then proceeded to top a century of points, sinking Tonga 101-10.

With prop Ngalu Taufo'ou sent off England punished the South Sea Islanders with a 13-try spectacular backed up by Paul Grayson's new national match record of 36 points from 12 conversions and four penalty goals.

Three men with a mission:
Left - Jonah Lomu (New Zealand)
Top - Diego Dominguez (Italy)
Bottom - Latiume Maka (Tonga)

England v Tonga: 'Epeli Taione takes on England's Worsley and Grewcock

THE 1999
RUGBY WORLD CUP

POOL C

France

Fiji

Canada

Namibia

France v Canada: Lineout at Béziers

It all rested on the final group match in Toulouse - and then it still went right down to the wire.

The third French try, scored by wing Christophe Dominici deep into injury time, clinched a 28-19 victory for France and earned them a direct passage into the last eight and a trip to Dublin while Fiji had to take on England at Twickenham for the right to a quarter-final place.

Fiji had got their noses in front but the French pack had too much firepower at a succession of close range scrums and referee Paddy O'Brien awarded a penalty try that swung it in the French favour.

France had hardly started their 1999 campaign before they had to come to

Fiji v Namibia: Clean possession for Fiji

terms with the loss of mercurial fly half Thomas Castaignède through a leg injury.

The Tricolours had stuttered into the tournament and things were hardly much rosier after they made hard work of beating Canada 33-20 in Béziers, the Canuks matching the home side for the best part of an hour only for Emile Ntamack to put France on the road to victory.

Ntamack struck with a try four minutes from the end after the 18,000 home crowd had resorted to whistling their concern when Canada had come back to within a point, courtesy of scrum half Morgan Williams' second try.

That was a superb solo effort from 30 metres out after Stephane Glas had got the luck of the bounce for the first of four French tries, the others coming from Olivier Magne and Castaignède.

Canada were not helped by the early departure of captain Gareth Rees - the only player to have appeared in all four World Cups - though John Tait was outstanding in the line-out.

Fiji had thrown down the group challenge on the Friday night by blitzing Namibia 67-18 at the same venue running in nine tries.

Backing up their slick handling was the boot of Waisale Serevi who contributed 22 points, including eight conversions.

Next up for Fiji was Canada in Bordeaux and they responded with arguably the most important win in their history, a 38-22 win after the Canuks had dominated the opening exchanges to build up an 11-point advantage.

But two tries just before half-time turned the match on its head - centre Viliame Satala grabbing two tries to earn himself a contract with Mont-de-Marsan into the bargain.

The one sour note was the red card shown to Marika Vunibaka in the final minute.

France failed to match Fiji's scoring feats against both Canada and Namibia, France having to be content with a 47-13 win over the African qualifiers in Bordeaux.

It was left to full back Ugo Mola, with a second half hat-trick of tries, to put some gloss on the French performance, centre Richard Dourthe ending up with 17 points from his boot.

There was delight and despair for Canada in their final match as they beat Namibia 72-11 but had flanker Dan Baugh sent off.

Rees was back for the finale and ended his 12-year love affair with the tournament by contributing 27 points to bow out with a 100 per cent kicking success rate this time. But with all hope gone of making it through to the knock-out stages it was left to France and Fiji to provide the final fireworks.

Fiji v Canada: Al Charron (Canada) accepts defeat

France v Fiji: Christophe Juillet scores France's opening try

France v Namibia: The French front row prepares for scrummage

France v Fiji: competing for the high ball

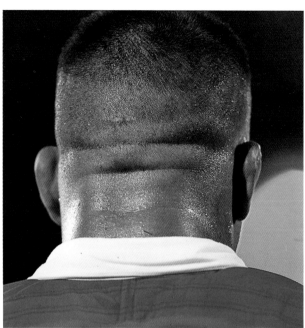

Must be a prop! France's Christian Califano

Fiji v Canada: Canada's Dave Lougheed challenges for the high ball

France v Namibia: Ugo Mola goes over for one of the French tries

THE 1999
RUGBY WORLD CUP

POOL D

Wales

Argentina

Samoa

Japan

Wales v Samoa
Lio Falaniko of Samoa scores one of his country's five tries

Wales reached the last eight for the first time since 1987 with Samoa going through to the play-offs from the "Group of Death" as runners-up - and Argentina also making it to the knock-out stages as the best of of the third placed teams.

In the tightest group of the lot all three finished with two wins and seven match points and it was left to the calculator to determine that Wales finished top after scoring 118 points to Samoa's 97 and Argentina's 83. Wales go straight into a Cardiff quarter-final showdown with Australia while Samoa and Argentina face play-offs against Ireland and Scotland.

After failing to make both the 1991 and 1995 quarter-finals, winning just one match each time, Wales failed to

make it three out of three when the Samoan jinx struck again as the team who had ruined their '91 hopes did their best to do so again with a 38-31 upset at the Millennium Stadium.

As hosts, Wales may have overdone the hospitality by gifting Pat Lam's team three of their five tries but there were no complaints from the Welsh camp at the end of their 10-Test winning run. Samoan scrum half Stephen Bachop had a superb match with the only Welsh celebrations coming in the shape of a new world points record for Neil Jenkins as he topped Michael Lynagh's 911 points.

The Welsh pack may have won the scrum battle, being awarded two penalty tries into the bargain, but Samoa won the war to leave the group one, two and three finishing positions hanging in the balance right until the final whistle of the Argentina-Japan clash.

That one ended in a 33-12 victory for the Pumas with fly half Gonzalo Quesada taking his tournament points tally to 66 with seven more penalty goals, opposite number Keiji Hirose accounting for all the Cherry Blossoms' points with four penalty goals of his own.

The occasion of the glittering opening ceremony at the new £126m Millennium Stadium had already seemed to get to the host nation as Rob Howley's team made a hesitant

start against Argentina.

Neil Jenkins missed his first penalty goal chance but he and Wales got it together to notch up a 23-18 win with tries from flanker Colin Charvis and centre Mark Taylor and 13 points from Jenkins.

The first citing incidents of the tournament ended in bans for Pumas prop Roberto Grau (three weeks) and Wales flanker Colin Charvis (two weeks).

The Pumas took all of 170 minutes to score their first try after fly half Gonzalo Quesada had kicked all 18 points against Wales and then the opening 18 against Samoa at Stradey Park.

Second row Alejandro Allub was the man to interrupt Quesada's scoring monopoly with a 70th minute try in

the 32-16 victory over the South Sea Islanders at Llanelli before it was back to business for the No 10 who ended up with just one miss in 10 attempts at goal.

The Samoans had looked impressive in blasting Japan to a 43-9 defeat at Wrexham, with wing Brian Lima collecting two of their five tries, but Wales easily surpassed that as the Cherry Blossoms were blown away 64-15 in front of yet another capacity Cardiff Arms Park crowd.

Taylor took his World Cup tally to three with two of the nine tries scored as Jenkins initially equalled Lynagh's individual points record with a 19-point tally before going on to take his tally to 927.

Wales v Japan: Ignacio Corleto of Argentina is upended

Wales v Japan: Hiroyuki Tanuma of Japan soars above the lineout

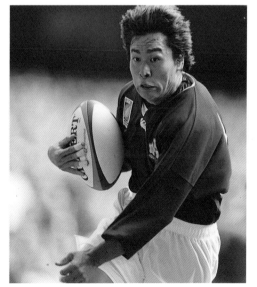
Wales v Japan: Daisuke Ohata (Japan) heads for the tryline

Wales v Japan: Craig Quinnell - selling the dummy

Wales v Samoa: Wales' Neil Jenkins overtakes Michael Lynagh's world record total of 911 international points

THE 1999
RUGBY WORLD CUP

POOL E

Australia

Ireland

IRISH RUGBY
FOOTBALL UNION

Romania

United States

Ireland v Australia
**RWC99's outstanding player Tim Horan
of Australia, dives to score**

Australia stormed into the quarter-finals with a 100 per cent record after beating chief challengers Ireland 23-3 in a bruising Lansdowne Road match.

That defeat consigned the Irish to a play-off against Argentina in Lens in their roundabout route and bid to make the quarter-finals.

The Wallabies had gone into the tournament on the back of a Tri Nations victory over New Zealand and a Belfast crowd of 12,500 was treated to nine Aussie tries as Romania went down 57-9.

Back row forward Toutai Kefu led the way with a hat-trick while wing Joe Roff snapped up a brace as the Romanians failed to breach the well organised Wallaby defence.

Ireland also topped a half century of points in their opener against the United States with the effervescent Keith Woods on song as the hooker forged his way over for four tries as the Eagles had their wings well and truly clipped.

While Woods was establishing a try scoring record for a hooker in an international - thanks to loitering out on the right wing for his fourth - in the main the Irish pack kept it tight as they coasted home 53-8.

The air was thick with citings after the Irish had seen their automatic last eight hopes disappear with Wallaby tries from Tim Horan and Ben Tune, plus 10 points from Matt Burke and three from skipper John Eales.

Ireland failed to find a way through the Australian defence and their only reward was a David Humphreys penalty goal from a match that ended up with Irish flanker Trevor Brennan and Aussies Kefu and centre Daniel Herbert all being cited. Brennan and Kefu were each banned for two matches while Herbert was cleared.

However, there was another blow to the Wallaby cause with the loss for the rest of the tournament of former captain Phil Kearns with a foot injury.

The Eagles' last chance of a tournament win as good as went when influential captain Dan Lyle was injured in the match against Romania in Dublin, a dislocated shoulder possibly ruling him out of action until

USA v Romania: Romania's Gheorghe Solomie kicks through

Ireland v Romania: Ireland's Andy Ward celebrates his try

Christmas.

The Eagles had gone 12 points clear shortly after half-time with a try by Brian Hightower, converted by Kevin Dalzell, but Romania upped their forward effort and a second try from Gheorghe Solomie put them back on course for victory.

With the top two places as good as signed, sealed and delivered, the Wallabies made hard work of seeing off the American Eagles 55-19 at Limerick while Ireland coasted home 44-14 against Romania in Dublin.

The Irish ran in five tries in killing off any lingering Romania hopes of further progress, captain Dion O'Cuinneagain getting the first and full back Conor O'Shea getting a brace as they booked their place on the flight to Lens.

Australia found the Eagles a tough nut to crack as the Americans went out in a blaze of defiance, making the largely second string Wallabies fight every inch of the way. The difference was just 15 points with 11 minutes to go before the Aussies stepped up a gear with two of their eight tries coming in injury time.

Matt Burke, playing out of position on the left wing, was one Wallaby who rose above the mediocre but while the three points went to the 1991 world champions, the honours went to captain Kevin Dalzell and his battling Eagles.

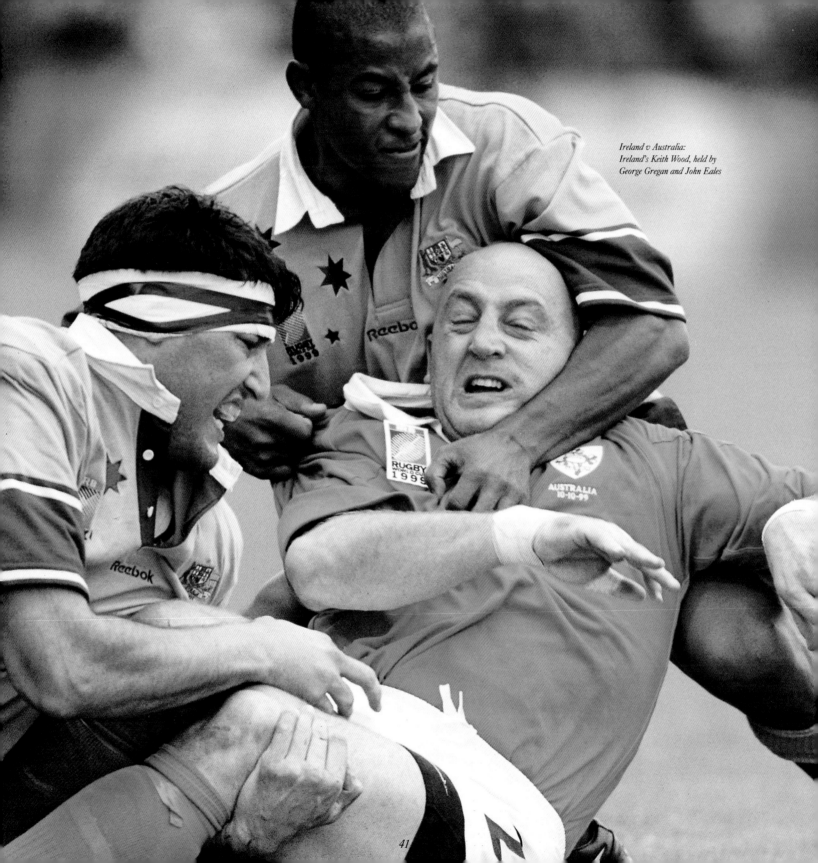

Ireland v Australia:
Ireland's Keith Wood, held by
George Gregan and John Eales

41

Ireland v Romania: Dion O'Cuinneagain leads in the line

Ireland v Australia: A try for Australia's Ben Tune

THE 1999
RUGBY WORLD CUP

Quarter Final Play-offs

 England v Fiji

Scotland v Samoa

 Ireland v Argentina

Ireland v Argentina
Diego Albanese's match-winning try for Argentina

Ireland v Argentina
Irish dejection – Argentinian celebration

Main picture

England v Fiji: One of "Larry's carries". Dallaglio on the charge

Top picture – England v Fiji: England's Neil Back offloads

Bottom Picture – A try for England's Dan Luger

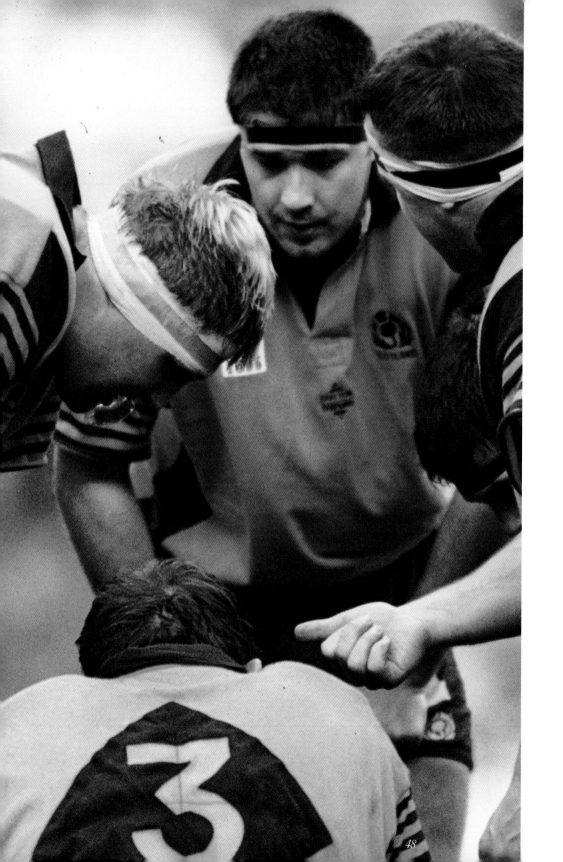

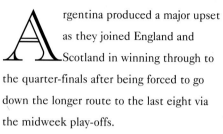

Argentina produced a major upset as they joined England and Scotland in winning through to the quarter-finals after being forced to go down the longer route to the last eight via the midweek play-offs.

The prize for Martin Johnson's team, who ended Fiji's interest in the tournament with a 45-24 victory at Twickenham, was a showdown with cup holders South Africa at Stade de France in Paris.

Scotland's 35-20 win over Samoa at Murrayfield earned them another outing at their Edinburgh home against 1987 cup winners New Zealand.

But Irish hopes of returning to Lansdowne Road were shattered as Argentina walked off 28-24 winners under the Lens floodlights to be the ones facing France in Dublin after possibly the greatest victory in Puma history.

England got the play-offs ball rolling by relying on three Jonny Wilkinson penalty goals in the first 20 minutes to provide a solid platform before wing Dan Luger sprinted over for a superb try, England attacking from deep inside their own half and producing some scintillating phase play.

With Fiji squandering several clear-cut chances, those misses looked even more costly when fly half Wilkinson caught them napping with a pinpoint kick out to the left that flanker Neil Back took magnificently on the burst for the second try.

Wing Nick Beal and Phil Greening got the other tries – hooker Greening declaring the match had been "hard graft" – with Wilkinson ending up with 23 points from seven penalty goals and a conversion. Wilkinson departed early after taking a knock, Matt Dawson getting his name on the scoresheet with a conversion.

There were three Fijian tries, from Viliame Satala, Imanueli Tikomaimakogai and Meli Nakauta, three Nicky Little penalty goals and a Waisale Serevi conversion, but England packed too much firepower.

"We did not play well," said England coach Clive Woodward. "Fiji played outstandingly well and we could have lost."

Meanwhile, Scotland opened their account against Samoa with a penalty try after the crowd had been subjected to scrum after scrum after scrum close to the Samoan line. Irish referee David McHugh finally tired of it all, wing Kenny Logan adding the conversion as he went about starting the business of notching up 17 more World Cup points.

Full back Silao Leaega got the South Sea Islanders on the board with a 25th minute penalty goal, but missed another chance of closing the gap further as he sent his next kick wide to the left.

The Scots pounded the Samoan line with some superb driving play with flanker Martin Leslie finally forcing his way over after fine spadework by prop Tom Smith and, although Logan missed the conversion, he made no mistake with a penalty goal minutes later – only for Leaega to promptly reply in kind.

However, three more Logan penalties, soon after half-time, opened up an 18-point lead and Smith made the inroads for fly half Gregor Townsend to land a drop goal to hammer the crucial nail in the Samoan coffin.

There was still time for flanker Semo Sititi and wing Brian Lima to cross for consolation tries, after powerful play from Va'aiga Tuigamala at the heart of their never-say-die performance.

But a fifth Logan penalty goal and wing Cameron Murray crossing for try No 3 for the Scots ensured that Samoa were comprehensively denied adding the Scottish scalp to the Welsh one they had taken in the big upset in the pool stage.

"We are satisfied with the performance and reaching the quarter-finals but we will have to play a lot better if we are to beat the All Blacks," said Townsend.

David Humphreys won "the battle of the boot" at Lens – but the Pumas won the war and were rewarded with their first quarter-final appearance courtesy of wing Diego Albanese's late, late try.

However, for the best part of 73 minutes it all revolved around fly halves Humphreys and Gonzalo Quesada as they displayed the goal kickers' craft with all eight of the first eight penalty goal attempts finding the mark.

It went Humphreys, Humphreys, Quesada, Humphreys, Quesada, Quesada, Humphreys and Humphreys – and when the Puma's No 10 missed collective chance No 9, in injury time, that was just about the biggest surprise of the first half.

The Pumas perhaps went closest with the ball in hand, flanker Rolando Martin prominent, while Irish hooker Keith Wood was into everything, displaying the sort of handling skills that brought him four tries against the United States.

It was back to business as usual after the break – though Humphreys did throw in a 44th minute drop goal by way of variety amongst the welter of penalties – as this time it went Humphreys, Humphreys, Quesada, Quesada, Humphreys and Quesada before a try came after precisely 72 minutes and 50 seconds.

Although held at an attacking scrum, the Pumas moved the ball wide and Albanese crossed for only their fourth try of the tournament but a priceless one – Quesada adding the conversion from wide out to leave the Irish trailing for the first time.

It was almost fitting that it ended in the manner it had began with Quesada sealing the Irish fate with his seventh penalty.

Fiji bid farewell to RWC99

THE 1999
RUGBY WORLD CUP

Quarter Finals

 Wales v Australia

South Africa v England

France v Argentina

New Zealand v Scotland

Wales v Australia

Australia marched into the Rugby World Cup semi-finals for the third time as they packed too much pace and skill for a revitalised Welsh team in front of a passionate 72,500 Millennium Stadium crowd.

The Wallabies, the 1999 Webb Ellis Trophy winners, failed to make it to the last four in 1995 but they produced the goods when it mattered most to knock out Wales and book their place at Twickenham and a Saturday showdown with South Africa.

John Eales' team outscored Wales three tries to none and have conceded just one try - to United States threequarter Juan Grobler - in 320 minutes of 1999 World Cup action.

Their mean defence was at it again in Cardiff, snuffing out the Wales attackers and forcing Wales into kicking to make any serious yardage in a thunderous contest that hung in the balance until the final 15 minutes.

That was when the Wallabies were the ones with the extra gas and in fly half Steve Larkham they had the ideal man to cash in and settle an absorbing tie with two late tries after Wales had clawed their way back to just a point adrift for fully 35 minutes.

The Wallabies had won the previous six meetings between the countries, going back to Wales' 22-21 victory in the 1987 RWC third place play-off in Rotorua, and they were clear favourites this time to make it seven on the trot.

The Aussies made just the start they wanted and the one Welsh fans feared when they scored the first of their three tries inside six minutes, Larkham doing the initial damage and wing Joe Roff having the pace to get around the Welsh defence and find scrum half George Gregan in support.

Gregan also got his second and the Wallabies' third, six minutes into second half injury time, but in between it was nip and tuck as Wales played with raw guts and courage against a side who were a class above.

Fly half Neil Jenkins got Wales off the mark with a superbly struck penalty goal from wide out on the left but the Aussie response was immediate.

Although they had not made the most of a chance with the ball in hand, a clear overlap going unexploited, full back Matt Burke, who had converted Gregan's try, was on target with his only penalty goal success of the match to push Australia seven points clear again.

Wales dug deep and Jenkins had no trouble cutting the deficit to that single point with straightforward penalties in the 20th and 30th minutes.

The next 35 minutes were pointless on the board but riveting stuff, Wales desperate to get their noses ahead and put doubts in Wallaby minds.

But that water-tight defence held firm and after 65 minutes Australia got the try that effectively took them into the last four and ended Wales' World Cup dream.

The astute Larkham put a delicate kick through the Welsh defence and wing Ben Tune skidded over the line, Burke converting that and Gregan's late, late effort to send the Wallabies to Twickenham.

South Africa v England

Jannie de Beer got the drop on England - five times to be exact - to maintain South Africa's 100 per

New Zealand v Scotland
Tana Umaga (New Zealand) and Scotland's Kenny Logan

Scotland coach, Jim Telfer retires from international rugby

Wales v Australia – Aerial combat

South Africa's Jannie de Beer drop-kicking England to defeat

cent World Cup record and clinch a Twickenham semi-final collision with fellow Southern Hemisphere giants and 1991 cup winners Australia.

The Springboks made it 10 out of 10 on the world stage as the defending champions put the boot into Martin Johnson's team in glorious sunshine at the Stade de France.

And the man with the biggest beam on his face was fly half de Beer as he broke record after record in the process of breaking English hearts and hopes.

De Beer helped himself to an international record five drop goals in the space of just 30 second half minutes and ended up with a new Springbok match mark of 34 points as England were blown away after the break and never able to crack a formidable green-jerseyed defence.

"It was just on, it was just one of those days and you have to take the opportunities when they are there," said de Beer, who was not even in the 'Boks original squad for their defence of the world title. How England must have wished he had stayed in a spectator's role.

England went behind for the first time in the 37th minute when South African captain Joost van der Westhuizen increased his own scrum half world try record to 29 and, if there was any element of doubt about his score as he squeezed in at the corner, there was nothing remotely suspect

Intent on success: Danny Grewcock (England), Olivier Magne (France) and George Gregan (Australia)

about the faultless right boot of de Beer.

It is worth noting his scoring sequence for posterity. It went: penalty (4 minutes); penalty (10); penalty (25); conversion (37); drop goal (44); drop goal (45); drop goal (54); drop goal (71); drop goal (74); penalty (78); penalty (+1); conversion (+3).

England fly half Paul Grayson kicked his first four penalty goal chances before sending No 5 wide to the right and it

was a poor clearance that sparked off van der Westhuizen's try as the Springboks ran the ball back with devastating effect.

Two more Grayson penalties kept them in touch at just four points adrift but when his next bounced back out off the crossbar, it then turned almost exclusively into the de Beer show.

Replacement Jonny Wilkinson missed his first scoring chance before finding

the target with a 63rd minute penalty but by then the 'Boks were bristling with confidence and de Beer simply could not put a foot wrong.

He even did the spadework for their second try in injury time, his cross field kick eluding everyone before taking a wicked bounce and falling obligingly into the waiting hands of Pieter Rossouw.

If there had been any question mark

over van der Westhuizen's try, de Beer made sure that his remarkable kicking – and his drop goal kicking in particular – was the issue for which this match will be best remembered.

It really was the afternoon that England's World Cup hopes had the boot put into them as the champions set up that fascinating Southern showdown.

France v Argentina

France, who finished in third place four years ago, made it back-to-back semi-final appearances as Argentina finally ran out of steam at Lansdowne Road and the Tricolours ensured a Sunday Twickenham clash with favourites New Zealand.

Raphäel Ibañez's team went off at a furious pace and were 17 points clear in just 10 minutes as the Pool C winners dominated the Pumas, who had arrived in Dublin via the longer play-off route and that sensational victory over Ireland.

Argentina came back strongly but that massive effort and extra match showed in the last quarter as France rattled up another 17 quick-fire points to finish with five tries and really get their World Cup show on the road while leaving the Pumas in despair after losing on their first appearance in the last eight.

Fly half, Christophe Lamaison got the opening points with a penalty goal

after Argentina had collapsed a scrum and then converted full back Xavier Garbajosa's sparkling first try when he even had the luxury of being able to ignore a man outside as the Pumas defence was shredded.

Gonzalo Quesada drew gasps of disbelief from the crowd when the Argentina No 10 actually proved human by missing his first penalty goal chance and worse followed when wing Philippe Bernat-Salles raced away for the second French try. Lamaison's conversion made it those 17 whirlwind points but the Pumas came back in style.

Scrum half, Agustin Pichot was the catalyst for the revival, darting around a close range scrum to force his way over despite the attentions of two defenders.

Quesada converted and added a penalty goal before the French made the most of some casual clearance work by skipper Lisandro Arbizu, Emile Ntamack charging his kick down and having the pace to get the crucial first touch. Lamaison's conversion and second penalty goal opened up the gap to 17 points for the second time.

Once again, back came the Pumas. Arbizu made amends for his earlier mistake by beating Ntamack all ends up as they ran a penalty for his side's second try with the boot of Quesada back in working order with another five points contribution.

Lamaison and Quesada proceeded to exchange penalties but with Ntamack

weaving some midfield magic it was far from being a kicking duel and when a late tackle earned the Pumas a prime attacking position full back Ignacio Corleto and play-off hero Diego Albanese had the French alarm bells ringing.

Quesada was replaced soon after passing the 100-point tournament barrier and a penalty goal from replacement Felipe Contepomi hardly represented fair reward for some magnificent Puma play as they took the game to the French, keeping the ball alive and displaying glorious close support and handling.

But Lamaison held his nerve with a long range penalty to keep a seven-point advantage and Bernat-Salles profited from great work by Garbajosa to cross for his second try and book France's place in the last four - though there was still time to apply the icing on the French cake with another Garbajosa try.

New Zealand v Scotland

New Zealand kept up their marvellous World Cup record of being the only country to make the semi-final stage in every tournament as they killed off the last hope of any UK interest in the last four by beating Scotland at a wet Murrayfield.

The clear-cut 1999 tournament favourites, and inaugural cup winners 12 years ago, booked their Sunday meeting with France by running in four tries in a display brimming with authority, patience and confidence in testing conditions.

This was the 21st meeting between the countries and Scotland have still to record a victory - a couple of draws the closest they have come. But there wasn't even the hint of them making it an historic first as the All Blacks hit the straps running.

With the public north of the border belatedly waking up to the tournament it was virtually all over – though the Scots gave it their all to the final whistle and "won" the second half 15-5 - as the All Blacks rattled up 17 points in better than even time with wing Tana Umaga and full back Jeff Wilson doing the damage.

An Andrew Mehrtens penalty had opened proceedings before Jonah Lomu and Christian Cullen were the providers for Umaga with Mehrtens doing the groundwork for Wilson to force his way over for his 38th Test try.

Mehrtens converted both and, although Kenny Logan gave the home fans something to cheer about with a penalty, Mehrtens was quick to cancel that out and then play his part in a magnificent combined defensive effort as Gary Armstrong's team threw everything at them.

And having weathered that storm it was almost inevitable that New Zealand would take advantage, Umaga duly doing just that with his second try deep

England captain, Martin Johnson

New Zealand v Scotland: Christian Cullen of New Zealand escapes the tackle of Glenn Metcalfe

Xavier Garbajosa (France) – on to the next hurdle

France v Argentina – the French win the lineout

into injury time for a 22-point cushion, the only relief for Scotland coming in the shape of a missed Wilson conversion.

Tony Brown took over at No 10 from a limping Mehrtens and, with the Scots giving it a real go and competing vigorously on the New Zealand line-out throw-in, Gregor Townsend drew first second half blood for the Scots with a simple drop goal to remind the All Blacks they still had willing opposition to deal with.

Superb defence denied Lomu in the left hand corner, and then by Glenn Metcalfe on one of the big man's trademark charges, but they could not do it a third time as a long pass from Josh Kronfeld gave him sight of the try line and that was all he needed for his sixth try of the tournament.

But still Scotland refused to buckle, pounding the Kiwi's line until flanker Budge Pountney finally found a way over for a deserved try converted by Logan.

There was another from wing Cameron Murray, albeit little more than consolation, and, while the All Blacks may not have finished as they had started, the conditions played a big part.

New Zealand had done the business when it mattered and simply left Scotland too high a mountain to climb while making it four out of four times in the last four.

THE 1999
RUGBY WORLD CUP

Semi Finals

 South Africa v Australia

 New Zealand v France

Australia v South Africa

The sizzling Southern showdown went all the way – and then some 20 minutes more – before Australia booked their place in a second World Cup final with a dramatic 27–21 extra time victory over defending champions South Africa at a wet but turbulent and high tension Twickenham.

After 10 straight wins it was the Springboks' first defeat in a World Cup match while the 1991 world champions walked off winners of a thriller that, although not through want of trying, did not produce a try but was always riveting stuff.

And what a time for a player to produce his first international drop goal – and with it the prize of taking on France in the final at Cardiff's Millennium Stadium.

At 18–18 at the end of bruising normal time the players had to dig deep for another big extra effort with fly half, Stephen Larkham, ending up the toast of Down Under with a 48 metre drop goal six minutes from the end of the 100 minutes that swung it the Wallabies' way when it really mattered.

It may have been the "Battle of the Boots" but with so much at stake and both teams raising their games another notch the contest was never less than totally absorbing.

With Aussie centre, Tim Horan, the most threatening runner on the pitch it was a day when the defences came out on top in a titanic struggle that was pure drama.

Wallaby full back, Matt Burke, had both the first and last words of the contest with penalty goals, his eighth moments after Larkham had got the drop on the Springboks putting the lid on matters.

"Of course we are disappointed," said South African coach, Nick Mallett, after John Eales' team had prised their hands off The Webb Ellis Cup. "But the team did not let themselves down, they have nothing to be ashamed about."

Opposite number, Rod Macqueen's brief team talk before going into those 20 minutes of extra time revolved around "calming down" after Springbok fly half, Jannie de Beer, had levelled matters deep into regulation injury time.

Burke had got the scoreboard ticking over with a couple of penalty goals, the second after one of Horan's clean breaks, before de Beer found his range from 45 metres.

For the rest of the first half it went Burke, de Beer and Burke – and there was more of the same after the break as South Africa turned to face the wind.

It took the Springboks just 11 minutes of the second period to draw level with another de Beer penalty and, by way of variety, his sixth drop goal of the tournament, before it returned to

South Africa v Australia – Australia's Daniel Herbert moves away from Bobby Skinstad's tap-tackle

Australia's captain, John Eales, rallies his troops (above)

South Africa v Australia – The biter bit! Stephen Larkham's astonishing drop goal (sequence below)

penalties in the order of Burke, Burke, de Beer and de Beer.

The Wallabies could, and should have, saved themselves from going the extra distance, a try by lock Eales being ruled out through a technicality and then scrum half, George Gregan, was penalised for not releasing when he was held up on the South African line.

But at 18–18 there was nothing else for it but to have a short break, regroup and play on, South Africa finally taking the lead for the first time three minutes after going into extra time with de Beer's sixth penalty goal.

Enter Larkham in a classic case of "cometh the hour, cometh the man." Coach Macqueen smilingly said of his huge drop goal "it was always going to be an ugly one" but when it cleared the bar with plenty to spare it was a priceless one and the 'Boks were left staring at their first defeat on the World Cup stage and the Wallabies were on their way to a second final.

New Zealand v France

There could have been a new name engraved on The Webb Ellis Cup after France produced the most sensational upset in World Cup history, coming back from being 14 points adrift with 33 unanswered points to beat red-hot favourites New Zealand 43-31 in the Sunday semi-final at Twickenham.

France, beaten by the All Blacks in

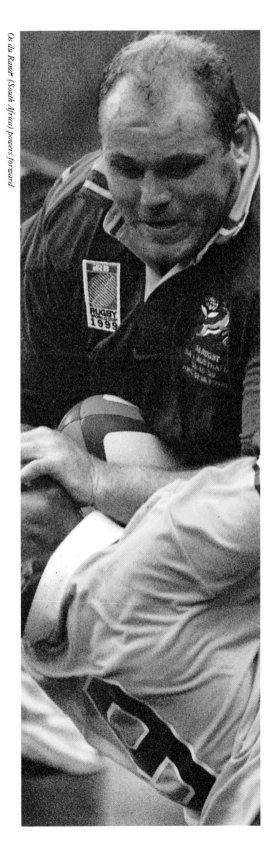

that inaugural final 12 years ago, gained ample revenge to earn the right to try and stop 1991 champions Australia making history by becoming the first country to win the coveted cup twice.

And they did it in style – scoring four tries to three with the two Christophes, fly half Lamaison and wing Dominici, in inspired form behind a pack who followed Abdel Benazzi's lead and simply refused to buckle.

France took the lead after just two minutes with a penalty goal from Lamaison with Andrew Mehrtens missing his first two penalty chances, first hitting the right upright and then sending his next sliding inches wide of the same post in what what was perhaps an omen of what was still to come.

It was third and fourth times lucky for the New Zealand fly half but back bounced Raphäel Ibañez's team to regain the lead with a gem of a try.

Wing, Christophe Dominici, who proved a real handful, did the spadework with one of the individual breaks of the tournament and when he was finally hauled down short the French won the vital ruck and had men to spare as Lamaison glided over

unchallenged for a try he converted to account for all 10 French points of the half.

Lamaison ended up with a 28-point tally but only after Mehrtens had added two more penalty goals in the opening half – sandwiching a Jonah Lomu "special" as he increased his own World Cup try record to the 14 mark in just two events.

Centre, Christian Cullen, flipped the ball on to the big man who had to stoop low to take control – and from then on it was all raw strength and determination as Lomu battled his way through half the French team to force his way over, leaving defenders littered in his wake.

Mehrtens missed the conversion and then was wide with another penalty goal chance as French captain Ibañez joined full back Xavier Garbajosa in being shown a yellow card.

If that wasn't bad enough, Lomu was at it again less than five minutes after the restart.

Full back, Jeff Wilson, took a wayward French kick in his own half and from innocuous beginnings came another superb try courtesy of a great

double act. The ball was switched from Wilson to Lomu, Lomu to Wilson and Wilson to Lomu before the powerhouse wing crashed over for his, and New Zealand's second try.

But then came perhaps the most remarkable comeback ever staged in such a vital match.

France began reminding the All Blacks they were anything but down and out as Lamaison struck with the boot six times in just 13 minutes as they turned the game on its head.

He kept the drop goal production line going with two more followed by a couple of penalty goals and then converted tries from Dominici and Richard Dourthe.

When wing, Dominici, collected Fabien Galthié's kick from a turnover for their second try and Dourthe did much the same from Lamaison's kick a 14 point New Zealand lead had been transformed into a 12 point French advantage in the blink of an eye.

There was still time for Philippe Bernat-Salles to claim France's fourth try and Wilson a consolation score for the All Blacks but the French celebrations had long since begun.

New Zealand v France – Lomu ghosts through (above)

Philippe Bernat-Salles – an interested observer

New Zealand v France – Philippe Bernat-Salles scores the clinhcing try for France

Christophe Lamaison (France)

France's Christophe Dominici held by Christian Cullen (above)

Franck Tournaire and Emile Ntamack (France) keeping it in the family

THE 1999
RUGBY WORLD CUP

Third & Fourth Place Play-off

 South Africa v New Zealand

The grim faces and body language of the supporters said it all – if the main guests at the main party two days later were someone else then they would rather be anywhere but Cardiff on a Thursday night and playing for the minor placings.

Both New Zealand and South Africa had strongly fancied their chances of becoming the first country to win the Webb Ellis Trophy twice but in the end they had to turn up at the Millennium Stadium some 44 hours ahead of their anticipated schedule with the only real prize the one of not having to go through the qualifying procedure for Australia 2003.

After 80 minutes of honest – after all, this was the 'Boks v the Blacks – if not spectacular endeavour, that crumb of comfort fell on the Springboks table as they won 22-18 in front of a crowd of nearly 65,000, leaving the mighty All Blacks to go through the process of qualifying for the next tournament.

South African fly half Henry Honiball was given one last appearance on the grand stage before departing the international scene and after an injury-

South Africa throw bodies at Jonah Lomu

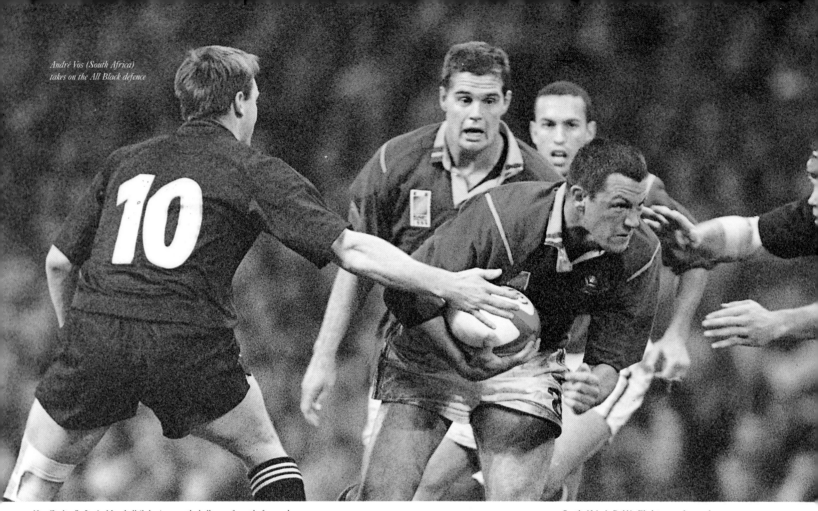

André Vos (South Africa) takes on the All Black defence

New Zealand's Justin Marshall (below) moves the ball away from the forwards

South Africa's Robbie Fleck powers forward

South Africa's Breyton Paulse kicks ahead to the score the game's only try

marred tournament at least he bowed out a winner after contributing half his side's points.

Which is more than could be said for New Zealand coach John Hart, who, after back-to-back defeats by France and the South Africans, announced the morning after the second sad event that he would not be seeking a continuation of his contract.

New Zealand were first to draw blood with a simple penalty goal from fly half Andrew Mehrtens after just eight minutes only for full back Percy Montgomery to level matters with the first of his two drop goals, albeit requiring the assistance of a kindly bounce off the crossbar.

Penalty goals from Honiball and Mehrtens kept it tight before wing Breyton Paulse – who proved that size isn't everything – gave the South African supporters real cause to celebrate.

The Western Province flyer kicked and chased from 70 metres out and when the ball squirted away from the covering Christian Cullen, Paulse pounced for what was to be the only try of the contest.

Honiball converted and added a second penalty goal but New Zealand made sure they stayed in touch with Mehrtens on target with two more penalties before the break.

The premature departure of Tana Umaga resulted in a re-shuffled All Blacks back division with Cullen switching to full back and Jeff Wilson to the wing.

But when Stefan Terblanche pulled off a thrilling tackle on Jonah Lomu, the Blacks must have known this was not going to be their day but rather one of those rare black days in their illustrious history.

Honiball made sure Taine Randell's team were always chasing the game with another penalty goal for a seven-point advantage but the All Blacks still refused to go out without a fight.

Mehrtens did claw back six more points with successful kicks that took his penalty haul to six but the 'Boks were not going to be denied, Montgomery finishing the South African scoring as he had started it with his second drop goal to save them from the ignominy of qualifying for 2003.

Springboks victorious

Airborne – Percy Montgomery of South Africa and All Black Christian Cullen

THE 1999
RUGBY WORLD CUP

The Final

 Australia v France

When John Eales raised the Webb Ellis Trophy high above his head in the Millennium Stadium, Cardiff, on 6th November, 1999, Australia had created Rugby World Cup history… the first country to win the game's most coveted prize twice.

The roll of honour now reads New Zealand, Australia, South Africa and Australia again and no-one present that historic day at the climax of the fourth tournament could dispute the Wallabies' right in becoming the first double world champions.

France – was their semi-final victory over New Zealand in reality their final? – were beaten 35-12 and this time the cup will stay put in Australia right through to the 2003 event. The practice of the winners passing the trophy on to the next host nation after a couple of years for promotional purposes means it will stay in Aussie hands until it all kicks-off again in Sydney in the first finals of the 21st century.

The Wallabies, who accounted for Ireland, Wales and reigning champions South Africa on their way to the showpiece occasion, lived up to their billing as red-hot final favourites and, when they put their foot on the gas in the final quarter, France knew it was all over some distance before the official finish.

With cricket's World Cup already under lock and key Down Under, Eales & Co were given a ticker-tape welcome as cup No 2 was safely brought home, albeit after a final that was built more around substance than style.

In truth, Australia squeezed the life out of the *Tricolours* as, yet again, the team with the best defence went on to lift the prize. Conceding just one try in 500 minutes of World Cup action (they were taken the extra 20 minutes distance by the Springboks) says it all about the Aussie class of '99.

France did have a chance or two, Abdel Benazzi called back for a forward pass after crossing Australia's line and Philippe Bernat-Salles denied by the outstanding Steve Larkham, but Australia were always in the driving seat.

For over an hour, however, the boot reigned supreme with the journey incidental and the arrival everything.

There were flashes of brilliance – Wallaby centre Tim Horan was both the man of the final as well as the man of the tournament – but there were seven penalty goals from the boot of Matt Burke to four from Christophe Lamaison.

However, the last of France's flickering hopes were well and truly extinguished in the 66th minute when Horan and Owen Finegan combined to send Ben Tune hurtling away for the first of their two tries.

The second was all raw power as Finegan resembled a runaway tank as he sent French defenders scattering, deep into injury time and, with Burke converting both, coach Rod Macqueen and Eales' team were assured of their niche in rugby folklore.

"We are very proud we have been part of our own history," said Eales, one of only three survivors from their 1991 winning side. "We have been talking about this for the last four years."

But they did the talking that really mattered when it mattered, out on the Millennium Stadium pitch, and it was entirely appropriate that it should all end with a delicious touch of irony.

On the day the Republicans lost the vote Down Under, staunch Republican Eales won the day in Wales and accepted the gold trophy from the Queen with the words "thank you very much your Majesty, this is a very special moment."

It certainly was.

Olivier Magne tackled by Owen Finegan (above)

*Well done, son! Richard Harry of Australia and his father,
ARU president Phil Harry (above)*

George Gregan of Australia, one of RWC99's outstanding performers (below)

Australia celebrate Ben Tune's try

Australia's Matt Cockbain and Fabien Galthie of France (above)

Richard Dourthe of France moves the ball to Emile Ntamack (below)

Australia's second try. Owen Finegan scores.

Joe Roff (Austrlia) is held up on the French try line

Australia's Tim Horan makes a typical break

The Holy Grail

Homecoming

THE 1999
RUGBY WORLD CUP

IN FOCUS

Chris Wyatt (Wales)
Another fine mess…

Cardiff

Llanelli

Stade de France

Béziers

Bordeaux

Twickenham

Lens

Huddersfield

Bristol

Leicester

Galashiels

Hampden Park, Glasgow

Murrayfield

Toulouse

Lansdowne Road, Dublin

Belfast

Limerick

Wrexham

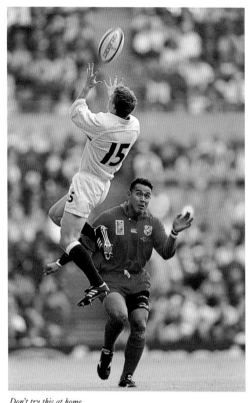

Don't try this at home

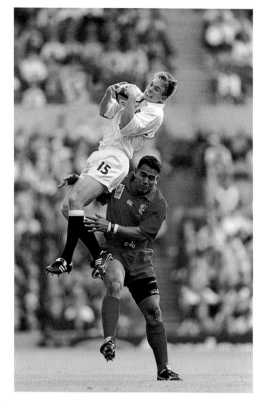

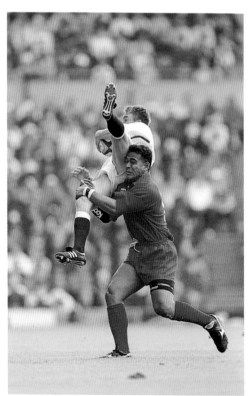

Xavier Garbajosa – broken heart

Olivier Magne – broken nose

Peter Marshall (Australia)

Chris White (England)

Joel Dumé (France)

Ed Morrison (England)

Stuart Dickinson (Australia)

Wayne Erickson (Australia)

Paul Honiss (New Zealand)

Derek Bevan (Wales)

Jim Fleming (Scotland)

Clayton Thomas (Wales)

Andrew Cole (Australia)

Paddy O'Brien (New Zealand)

Colin Hawke (New Zealand)

Brian Campsall (England)

David McHugh (Ireland)

André Watson (South Africa)

The Whistle Blowers

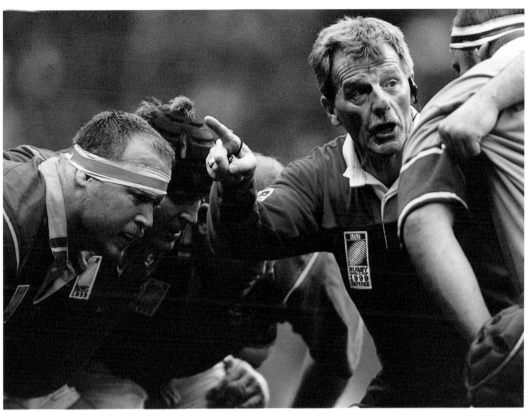

Wales' Derek Bevan makes a point

RWC99 photocall; Referees and Touch Judges

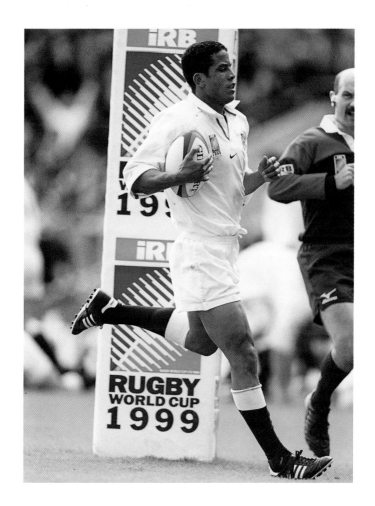

Jeremy Guscott, of England,
announced his retirement
from international
rugby during RWC99

The date: 6th November 1999
The place: The Millennium Stadium, Cardiff
The occasion: Closing Ceremony Rugby World Cup 1999

THE 1999
RUGBY WORLD CUP

STATISTICAL REVIEW

THE POOL MATCHES

Pool A

2 October, Netherdale, Galashiels

SPAIN........................15 (5PG)
URUGUAY 27 (2G 1PG 2T)

Deon Kayser (South Africa)

Spain: MA Frechilla; O Ripol, A Enciso, S Loubsens, R Bastide; A Kovalenco, J Alonso; J Camps, F de la Calle, JI Zapatero, J-M Villau, S Souto, J Diaz, A Malo *(captain)*, C Souto
Substitutions: O Astarloa for S Souto (65 mins); D Zarzosa for de la Calle (65 mins); A Mata for Diaz (81 mins)
Scorer: Penalty Goals: Kovalenco (5)
Uruguay: A Cardoso; M Ferres, P Vecino, M Mendaro, P Costabile; D Aguirre, F Sciarra; R Sanchez, D Lamelas, P Lemoine, J C Bado, M Lame, N Brignoni, D Ormaechea *(captain)*, M Panizza

Substitutions: N Grille for Brignoni (65 mins); A Ponce de Lion for Lame (65 mins); F Sosa Diaz for Sciarra (70 mins); F de los Santos for Lamelas (73 mins); G Storace for Lemoine (73 mins); J Menchaca for Aguirre (80 mins)
Scorers: Tries: Ormaechea, penalty try, Cardoso, Menchaca *Conversions:* Aguirre, Sciarra *Penalty Goal:* Aguirre
Referee: C White (England)

3 October, Murrayfield

SOUTH AFRICA....46 (5G 2PG 1T)
SCOTLAND 29 (2G 4PG 1DG)

South Africa: PC Montgomery; DJ Kayser, RF Fleck, B Venter, PWG Rossouw; JH de Beer, JH van der Westhuizen *(captain)*; JP du Randt, AE Drotské, IJ Visagie, PA van den Berg, MG Andrews, JC Erasmus, RB Skinstad, AG Venter
Substitutions: A-H le Roux for du Randt (47 mins); K Otto for Andrews (47 mins); BP Paulse for Kayser (70 mins); AN Vos for Erasmus (81 mins)
Scorers: Tries: B Venter, Fleck, A Venter, le Roux, Kayser, van der Westhuizen
Conversions: de Beer (5) *Penalty Goals:* de Beer (2)
Scotland: GH Metcalfe; CA Murray, AV Tait, JA Leslie, KM Logan; GPJ Townsend, G Armstrong *(captain)*; TJ Smith, GC Bulloch, G Graham, S Murray, SB Grimes, MD Leslie, GL Simpson, AC Pountney
Substitutions: MJM Mayer for J Leslie (54 mins); P Walton for Simpson (61 mins); GW Weir for S Murray (72 mins); DIW Hilton for Graham (73 mins)
Scorers: Tries: M Leslie, Tait
Conversions: Logan (2) *Penalty Goals:* Logan (4)
Dropped Goal: Townsend
Referee: C J Hawke (New Zealand)

8 October, Murrayfield

SCOTLAND 43 (5G 1PG 1T)
URUGUAY 12 (4PG)

Scotland: GH Metcalfe; CA Murray, AV Tait, MJM Mayer, KM Logan; GPJ Townsend, G Armstrong *(captain)*; TJ Smith, GC Bulloch, G Graham, S Murray, SB Grimes, MD Leslie, GL Simpson, AC Pountney
Substitutions: BW Redpath for Armstrong (58 mins); DIW Hilton for Graham (64 mins); RR Russell for Bulloch (70 mins); P Walton for Leslie (74 mins); SL Longstaff for C Murray (79 mins)
Scorers: Tries: M Leslie, Armstrong, Simpson, Townsend, Metcalfe, Russell
Conversions: Logan (5) *Penalty Goal:* Logan
Uruguay: A Cardoso; J Menchaca, P Vecino, M Mendaro, P Costabile; D Aguirre, F Sciarra; R Sanchez, D Lamelas, P Lemoine, J C Bado, M Lame, N Brignoni, D Ormaechea *(captain)*, M Panizza
Substitutions: F Sosa Diaz for Sciarra (HT); N Grille for Brignoni (59 mins); E Berruti for Sanchez (62 mins); A Ponce de Lion for Lame (65 mins); F de los Santos for Lamelas (70 mins); G Storace for Lemoine (70 mins); J Viana for Aguirre (77 mins)
Scorers: Penalty Goals: Aguirre (3), Sciarra
Referee: S Dickinson (Australia)

10 October, Murrayfield

SOUTH AFRICA....47 (6G 1T)
SPAIN........................3 (1PG)

South Africa: BJ Paulse; CS Terblanche, W Julies, PG Muller, K Malotana; JH de Beer, W Swanepoel; A-H le Roux, CLC Rossouw, AC Garvey, FJ van Heerden,

Jannie de Beer (South Africa) and Glenn Metcalfe (Scotland)

K Otto, RJ Kruger, AN Vos *(captain)*,
A Leonard

Substitutions: DJ Kayser for Julies (22 mins);
JH van der Westhuizen for Swanepoel (62
mins); RB Skinstad for Leonard (62 mins);
JP du Randt for le Roux (65 mins); AE
Drotské for Rossouw (65 mins)

Scorers: Tries: Vos (2), Swanepoel, Leonard,
penalty try, Muller, Skinstad

Conversions: de Beer (6)

Spain: F Puertas; J-I Inchausti, A Socias,
F Diez, MA Frechilla; A Etxeberria,
A Gallastegui; J Camps, D Zarzosa,
JI Zapatero, J-M Villau, O Astarloa, J Diaz,
A Malo *(captain)*, C Souto

Substitutions: V Torres for Camps (20 mins);
A Mata for Malo (43 mins); F Velazco for
Etxeberria (47 mins); F de la Calle for
Zarzosa (62 mins); L Javier Martinez for
Souto (67 mins)

Scorer: Penalty Goal: Velazco

Referee: P J Honiss (New Zealand)

15 October, Hampden Park, Glasgow

SOUTH AFRICA....39 (4G 2PG 1T)
URUGUAY 3 (1PG)

South Africa: PC Montgomery; DJ Kayser,
RF Fleck, B Venter, PWG Rossouw;
JH de Beer, JH van der Westhuizen *(captain)*;
JP du Randt, AE Drotské, IJ Visagie, K Otto,
MG Andrews, JC Erasmus, RB Skinstad,
AG Venter

Substitutions: A-H le Roux for Visagie (temp 2
to 11 mins) and for du Randt (51 mins);
PA van den Berg for Andrews (67 mins)

Scorers: Tries: van den Berg (2), Fleck,
Kayser, van der Westhuizen *Conversions:* de
Beer (4) *Penalty Goals:* de Beer (2)

Sent off: B. Venter

Uruguay: A Cardoso; J Menchaca, P Vecino,
F Paullier, P Costabile; D Aguirre, F Sosa
Diaz; R Sanchez, D Lamelas, P Lemoine,
JC Bado, M Lame, N Grille, D Ormaechea
(captain), M Panizza

Substitutions: S Aguirre for D Aguirre (temp

13 to 20 mins) and for Paullier (20 mins); N
Brignoni for Panizza (56 mins); E Berruti for
Sanchez (67 mins); G Storace for Lemoine
(67 mins); J Viana for Menchaca (78 mins);
J Alzueta for Lame (78 mins)

Scorer: Penalty Goal: D Aguirre

Referee: P Marshall (Australia)

16 October, Murrayfield

SCOTLAND 48 (5G 1PG 2T)
SPAIN.........................0

Scotland: C Paterson; CA Murray,
MJM Mayer, JG McLaren, SL Longstaff;
DW Hodge, BW Redpath *(captain)*;
DIW Hilton, RR Russell, AP Burnell,
GW Weir, AI Reed, P Walton, SJ Reid,
CG Mather

Substitutions: GPJ Townsend for McLaren
(76 mins); IT Fairley for Redpath (76 mins)

Scorers: Tries: Mather (2), C Murray,
McLaren, Longstaff, penalty try, Hodge
Conversions: Hodge (5) *Penalty Goal:* Hodge

Spain: F Puertas; J-I Inchausti, A Enciso
(captain), S Loubsens, MA Frechilla;
A Kovalenco, A Gallastegui; V Torres,
D Zarzosa, JI Zapatero, J-M Villau,
O Astarloa, J Diaz, A Mata, C Souto

Substitutions: L Javier Martinez for Torres
(HT); A Socias for Inchausti (48 mins);
F Velazco for Puertas (49 mins); S Tuineau
for Astarloa (57 mins); A Malet for Souto
(69 mins); F de la Calle for Zarzosa (76 mins)

Referee: C Thomas (Wales)

POOL A FINAL TABLE

	P	W	D	L	F	A	Pts
South Africa	3	3	0	0	132	35	9
Scotland	3	2	0	1	120	58	7
Uruguay	3	1	0	2	42	97	5
Spain	3	0	0	3	18	122	3

Pool B

2 October, Twickenham

ENGLAND 67 (6G 5PG 2T)

ITALY 7 (1G)

England: MB Perry; A S Healey, WJH Greenwood, PR de Glanville, DD Luger; JP Wilkinson, MJS Dawson; J Leonard, R Cockerill, PJ Vickery, MO Johnson *(captain)*, DJ Grewcock, RA Hill, LBN Dallaglio, NA Back

Substitutions: JC Guscott for Greenwood (35 mins); PBT Greening for Cockerill (56 mins); GC Rowntree for Leonard (65 mins); DJ Garforth for Vickery (65 mins); ME Corry for Grewcock (78 mins); ND Beal for Perry (78 mins)

Scorers: Tries: Perry, de Glanville, Luger, Wilkinson, Dawson, Hill, Back, Corry

Conversions: Wilkinson (6) *Penalty Goals:* Wilkinson (5)

Italy: MJ Pini; P Vaccari, AC Stoica, L Martin, N Zisti; D Dominguez, A Troncon; P Pucciariello, A Moscardi, F Properzi-Curti, W Cristofoletto, M Giacheri, M Giovanelli *(captain)*, O Arancio, M Bergamasco

Substitutions: A de Rossi for Bergamasco (18 mins); N Mazzucato for Pini (20 mins); C Checchinato for Cristofoletto (54 mins); F Mazzariol for Dominguez (76 mins)

Scorer: Try: Dominguez

Conversion: Dominguez

Referee: A Watson (South Africa)

England v New Zealand

3 October, Ashton Gate, Bristol

NEW ZEALAND 45 (4G 4PG 1T)

TONGA 9 (3PG)

New Zealand: JW Wilson; TJF Umaga, CM Cullen, A Ieremia, JT Lomu; AP Mehrtens, JW Marshall; CH Hoeft, AD Oliver, KJ Meeuws, NM Maxwell, RM Brooke, RD Thorne, TC Randell *(captain)*, JA Kronfeld

Substitutions: CW Dowd for Meeuws (11 mins); BT Kelleher for Marshall (63 mins); DPE Gibson for Ieremia (67 mins); RK Willis for Maxwell (69 mins)

Scorers: Tries: Lomu (2), Kronfeld, Maxwell, Kelleher *Conversions:* Mehrtens (4)

Penalty Goals: Mehrtens (4)

Tonga: S Taumalolo; F Tatafu, T Tiueti, S Taupeaafe, T Taufahema; E Vunipola *(captain)*, S Martens; T Faiga'anuku, F Vunipola, T Taumoepeau, I Fatani, BH Kivalu, V Fakatou, V Toloke, S Koloi

Substitutions: F Mafi for Kivalu (HT); D Edwards for Koloi (HT); I Tapueluelu for Tiueti (54 mins); N Ta'ufo'ou for Faiga'anuku (54 mins); M Te Pou for Toloke (69 mins); SM Tu'ipulotu for Martens (77 mins); L Maka for F Vunipola (78 mins)

Scorer: Penalty Goals: Taumalolo (3)

Referee: W D Bevan (Wales)

9 October, Twickenham

ENGLAND 16 (1G 3PG)

NEW ZEALAND 30 (3G 3PG)

England: MB Perry; AS Healey, PR de Glanville, JC Guscott, DD Luger; JP Wilkinson, MJS Dawson; J Leonard, R Cockerill, PJ Vickery, MO Johnson *(captain)*, DJ Grewcock, RA Hill, LBN Dallaglio, NA Back

Substitutions: DJ Garforth for Vickery (53 mins); TAK Rodber for Grewcock (60 mins); PBT Greening for Cockerill (71 mins); PJ Grayson for Wilkinson (71 mins); ME Corry for Hill (temp 12 to 18 mins) and for Back (81 mins)

Scorers: Try: de Glanville

Conversion: Wilkinson *Penalty Goals:* Wilkinson (3)

New Zealand: JW Wilson; TJF Umaga, CM Cullen, A Ieremia, JT Lomu; AP Mehrtens, JW Marshall; CH Hoeft, AD Oliver, CW Dowd, NM Maxwell, RM Brooke, RD Thorne, TC Randell *(captain)*, JA Kronfeld

Substitutions: BT Kelleher for Marshall (64 mins); RK Willis for Brooke (65 mins); DPE Gibson for Ieremia (68 mins); TE Brown for Mehrtens (81 mins);

Tony Brown (New Zealand)

GE Feek for Dowd (temp 29 to 31 mins and 39 mins to HT)

Scorers: Tries: Wilson, Lomu, Kelleher

Conversions: Mehrtens (3)

Penalty Goals: Mehrtens (3)

Referee: P Marshall (Australia)

10 October, Welford Road, Leicester

ITALY.................**25** **(1G 6PG)**
TONGA...............**28** **(2G 2PG 1DG 1T)**

Italy: MJ Pini; P Vaccari, AC Stoica, A Ceppolino, F Roselli; D Dominguez, A Troncon; A Moreno, A Moscardi, A Castellani, C Checchinato, M Giacheri, M Giovanelli *(captain)*, C Caione, S Saviozzi
Substitutions: A Moretti for Moscardi (69 mins); F Properzi-Curti for Moreno (82 mins); N Mazzucato for Vaccari (82 mins)
Scorers: Try: Moscardi *Conversion:* Dominguez
Penalty Goals: Dominguez (6)

Tonga: S Tu'ipulotu; T Taufahema, S Taupeaafe, E Vunipola *(captain)*, E Taione; B Woolley, S Martens; T Faiga'anuku, L Maka, N Ta'ufo'ou, F Mafi, B H Kivalu, D Edwards, K Tu'ipulotu, S Koloi
Substitutions: T Tiueti for Woolley (17 mins); I Fatani for Mafi (HT); I Tapueluelu (51 mins); M Te Pou for K Tu'ipulotu (77 mins)
Scorers: Tries: Taufahema, S Tu'ipulotu, Fatani *Conversions:* S Tu'ipulotu (2) *Penalty Goals:* S Tu'ipulotu (2) *Dropped Goal:* S Tu'ipulotu
Referee: D T M McHugh (Ireland)

14 October, Alfred McAlpine Stadium, Huddersfield

NEW ZEALAND ..101 **(11G 3PG 3T)**
ITALY.........................**3** **(1PG)**

New Zealand: JW Wilson; GM Osborne, PF Alatini, DPE Gibson, JT Lomu; TE Brown, BT Kelleher; GE Feek, MG Hammett, CW Dowd, ID Jones, RK Willis, DG Mika, TC Randell *(captain)*, AF Blowers

Substitutions: RJ Duggan for Kelleher (58 mins); SM Robertson for Blowers (58 mins); KJ Meeuws for Feek (64 mins); CM Cullen for Randell (74 mins); RM Brooke for Willis (76 mins)
Scorers: Tries: Wilson (3), Lomu (2), Osborne (2), Brown, Mika, Randell, Gibson, Robertson, Cullen, Hammett *Conversions:* Brown (11) *Penalty Goals:* Brown (3)

Italy: MJ Pini; P Vaccari, AC Stoica, A Ceppolino, N Zisti; D Dominguez, A Troncon; A Moreno, A Moretti, A Castellani, C Checchinato, M Giacheri, M Giovanelli *(captain)*, C Caione, S Saviozzi
Substitutions: N Mazzucato for Vaccari (8 mins); F Mazzariol for Dominguez (HT); A Moscardi for Moretti (HT); F Properzi Curti for Castellani (HT); O Arancio for Caione (50 mins); W Cristofoletto for Checchinato (67 mins)
Scorer: Penalty Goal: Dominguez
Referee: J M Fleming (Scotland)

Sililo Martens (Tonga)

England's Dan Luger, against Tonga

15 October, Twickenham

ENGLAND 101 (12G 4PG 1T)
TONGA 10 (1G 1PG)

England: MB Perry; AS Healey, WJH Greenwood, JC Guscott, DD Luger; PJ Grayson, MJS Dawson; GC Rowntree, PBT Greening, PJ Vickery, MO Johnson *(captain)*, GS Archer, JPR Worsley, LBN Dallaglio, RA Hill

Substitutions: ND Beal for Dawson (31 mins); DJ Grewcock for Johnson (50 mins); MJ Catt for Greenwood (50 mins); R Cockerill for Dallaglio (59 mins)

Scorers: Tries: Greening (2), Luger (2), Greenwood (2), Healey (2), Guscott (2), Hill, Dawson, Perry *Conversions:* Grayson (12) *Penalty Goals:* Grayson (4)

Tonga: S Tu'ipulotu; T Tiueti, F Tatafu, S Finau, S Taupeaafe; E Vunipola *(captain)*, S Martens; N Ta'ufo'ou, F Vunipola, T Taumoepeau, I Fatani, BH Kivalu, D Edwards, K Tu'ipulotu, S Koloi

Substitutions: T Faiga'anuku for Edwards (38 mins); F Mafi for K Tu'ipulotu (HT); I Tapueluela (temp for F Vunipola 31 to 43 mins) and for S Tu'ipulotu (53 mins); E Taione for Taupeaafe (58 mins);

SM Tu'ipulotu for Martens (58 mins); V Toloke for Kivalu (60 mins); L Maka for F Vunipola (69 mins)

Scorers: Try: Tiueti *Conversion:* S Tu'ipulotu
Penalty Goal: S Tu'ipulotu
Sent Off: N. Ta'ufo'ou

Referee: W J Erickson (Australia)

POOL B FINAL TABLE							
	P	W	D	L	F	A	Pts
New Zealand	3	3	0	0	176	28	9
England	3	2	0	1	184	47	7
Tonga	3	1	0	2	47	171	5
Italy	3	0	0	3	35	196	3

Waisele Serevi (Fiji)

Pool C

1 October, Stade de la Méditerranée, Béziers

FIJI 67 (8G 2PG 1T)
NAMIBIA 18 (1G 2PG 1T)

Fiji: A Uluinayau; F Lasagavibau, V Satala, W Sotutu, I Tikomaimakogai; W Serevi, J Rauluni; D Rouse, G Smith *(captain)*, J Veitayaki, S Raiwalui, E Katalau, A Naevo, A Mocelutu, S N Tawake

Substitutions: E Naituivau for Veitayaki (46 mins); M Nakatau for Sotutu (53 mins); K Sewabu for Mocelutu (68 mins); N Little for Lasagavibau (72 mins)

Scorers: Tries: Lasagavibau (2), Tikomaimakogai, Katalau, S Tawake, Satala, Mocelutu, Smith, J Rauluni *Conversions:* Serevi (8) *Penalty Goals:* Serevi (2)

Namibia: L van Dyk; D Farmer, A Samuelson, S van der Merwe, D Mouton; J Zaayman, R Jantjies; M Jacobs, H Horn, G Opperman, H Senekal, P Steyn, Q Hough *(captain)*, S Furter, J Olivier

Substitutions: G van Wyk for Mouton (HT); F J van Rensburg for Farmer (48 mins); E Smith for Horn (58 mins); A Blaauw for Opperman (58 mins); J Theron for Senekal (temp 20-28 mins) and for Steyn (65 mins); H Lintvelt for Olivier (65 mins); SJ van Rensburg for Zaayman (74 mins)

Scorers: Tries: Senekal, Jacobs *Conversion:* van Dyk *Penalty Goals:* van Dyk (2)

Referee: D T M McHugh (Ireland)

2 October, Stade de la Méditerranée, Beziers

FRANCE **33** (2G 3PG 2T)

CANADA **20** (2G 2PG)

France: U Mola; X Garbajosa, R Dourthe, S Glas, C Dominici; T Castaignède, P Mignoni; C Califano, R Ibañez *(captain)*, F Tournaire, A Benazzi, F Pelous, M Lièvremont, C Juillet, O Magne

Substitutions: C Lamaison for Mola (55 mins); O Brouzet for Pelous (72 mins); E Ntamack for Garbajosa (72 mins); S Castaignède for Mignoni (78 mins); C Soulette for Califano (78 mins); L Mallier for M Lièvremont (78 mins)

Scorers: Tries: Glas, Magne, Garbajosa, Ntamack *Conversions:* Dourthe (2) *Penalty Goals:* Dourthe (3)

Canada: DS Stewart; W Stanley, DC Lougheed, S Bryan, C Smith; GL Rees *(captain)*, M Williams; RGA Snow, P Dunkley, J Thiel, J Tait, MB James, JR Hutchinson,

Scott Stewart (Canada)

AJ Charron, D Baugh

Substitutions: RP Ross for Rees (41 mins); R Bice for Thiel (54 mins); R Banks for Hutchinson (62 mins); M Schmid for Tait (70 mins); JD Graf for Williams (73 mins)

Scorers: Tries: Williams (2) *Conversions:* Rees, Ross *Penalty Goals:* Rees, Ross

Referee: B Campsall (England)

8 October, Parc Lescure, Bordeaux

FRANCE **47** (4G 3PG 2T)

NAMIBIA **13** (1G 2PG)

France: U Mola; P Bernat-Salles, R Dourthe, S Glas, E Ntamack; C Lamaison, P Mignoni; C Califano, R Ibañez *(captain)*, F Tournaire, O Brouzet, F Pelous, M Lièvremont, T Lièvremont, O Magne

Substitutions: A Benazzi for T Lièvremont (25 mins); C Desbrosse for Glas (42 mins); A Costes for Magne (61 mins); C Soulette for Califano (66 mins); M Dal Maso for Ibañez

(66 mins); X Garbajosa for Mola (70 mins); S Castaignède for Mignoni (75 mins)

Scorers: Tries: Mola (3), Mignoni, Bernat-Salles, Ntamack *Conversions:* Dourthe (4) *Penalty Goals:* Dourthe (3)

Namibia: G Van Wyk; L van Dyk, FJ van Rensburg, S van der Merwe, A Samuelson; J Zaayman, R Jantjies; M Jacobs, H Horn, G Opperman, H Senekal, P Steyn, Q Hough *(captain)*, S Furter, M van Rooyen

Substitutions: E Smith for Jacobs (33 mins); H Lintvelt for van Rooyen (55 mins); J Theron for Steyn (56 mins); S J van Rensburg for Jantjies (63 mins); C Loubser for F van Resnburg (64 mins); A Blaauw for Opperman (67 mins)

Scorers: Try: Samuelson *Conversion:* van Dyk *Penalty Goals:* van Dyk (2)

Referee: C White (England)

9 October, Parc Lescure, Bordeaux

FIJI **38** (3G 3PG 1DG 1T)

CANADA **22** (1G 4PG 1DG)

Fiji: A Uluinayau; F Lasagavibau, V Satala, W Sotutu, M Vunibaka; N Little, J Rauluni; D Rouse, G Smith *(captain)*, J Veitayaki, S Raiwalui, E Katalau, IS Tabua, A Mocelutu, SN Tawake

Substitutions: W Serevi for Uluinayau (HT); K Sewabu for Mocelutu (HT); A Naevo for Tabua (69 mins); M Rauluni for J Rauluni (77 mins)

Scorers: Tries: Satala (2), penalty try, Vunibaka *Conversions:* Little (3) *Penalty Goals:* Little (3) *Drop Goal:* Little

Sent off: Vunibaka

Canada: D S Stewart; W Stanley, K Nichols, S Bryan, DC Lougheed; GL Rees *(captain)*,

M Williams; RGA Snow, P Dunkley, J Thiel, J Tait, MB James, AJ Charron, M Schmid, D Baugh

Substitutions: ME Cardinal for Dunkley (55 mins); D Major for Thiel (62 mins); JR Hutchinson for Schmid (62 mins); P Dunkley for Cardinal (71 mins)

Scorer: Try: penalty try *Conversion:* Rees *Penalty Goals:* Rees (4) *Dropped Goal:* Rees

Referee: EF Morrison (England)

14 October, Stade Municipal, Toulouse

CANADA **72** (9G 3PG)
NAMIBIA **11** (2PG 1T)

Canada: DS Stewart; W Stanley, DC Lougheed, K Nichols, J Pagano; GL Rees *(captain)*, M Williams; RGA Snow, ME Cardinal, J Thiel, J Tait, MB James, JR Hutchinson, AJ Charron, D Baugh

Substitutions: P Dunkley for Cardinal (48 mins); D Major for Thiel (62 mins); RP Ross for Pagano (64 mins); R Banks for Hutchinson (71 mins); S Bryan for Lougheed (71 mins); M Schmid for Tait (79 mins); JD Graf for Stewart (84 mins)

Scorers: Tries: Nichols (2), Snow (2), Stanley (2), Charron, Williams, Ross *Conversions:* Rees (9) *Penalty Goals:* Rees (3)

Sent off: Baugh

Namibia: G Van Wyk; L van Dyk, FJ van Rensburg, S van der Merwe, A Samuelson; J Zaayman, R Jantjies; E Smith, H Horn, G Opperman, H Senekal, P Steyn, Q Hough *(captain)*, S Furter, M van Rooyen

Substitutions: H Lintvelt for van Rooyen (HT); J Theron for Steyn (HT); A Blaauw for Opperman (HT); G Opperman for Smith (68 mins)

Scorers: Try: Hough *Penalty Goals:* van Dyk (2)

Referee: A Cole (Australia)

16 October, Stade Municipal, Toulouse

FRANCE **28** (2G 3PG 1T)
FIJI **19** (1G 4PG)

France: U Mola; P Bernat-Salles, R Dourthe, E Ntamack, C Dominici; C Lamaison, S Castaignède; C Califano, R Ibañez *(captain)*, F Tournaire, A Benazzi, F Pelous, M Lièvremont, C Juillet, O Magne

Substitutions: M Dal Maso for Ibañez (51 mins); X Garbajosa for Mola (55 mins); O Brouzet for Juillet (64 mins); F Galthié for Castaignède (71 mins); A Costes for Magne (75 mins)

Scorers: Tries: Juillet, penalty try, Dominici *Conversions:* Dourthe (2) *Penalty Goals:* Dourthe (2), Lamaison

Fiji: A Uluinayau; F Lasagavibau, V Satala, W Sotutu, M Bari; N Little, J Rauluni; D Rouse, G Smith *(captain)*, J Veitayaki, S Raiwalui, E Katalau, I S Tabua, A Mocelutu, SN Tawake

Substitutions: K Sewabu for Tabua (temp HT to 48 mins) and for Mocelutu (48 mins); M Nakauta for Bari (55 mins)

Scorers: Try: Uluinayau *Conversions:* Little *Penalty Goals:* Little (4)

Referee: P D O'Brien (New Zealand)

POOL C FINAL TABLE							
	P	W	D	L	F	A	Pts
France	3	3	0	0	108	52	9
Fiji	3	2	0	1	124	68	7
Canada	3	1	0	2	114	82	5
Namibia	3	0	0	3	42	186	3

Stephane Castaignède (France)

Arthur Samuelson (Namibia)

Colin Charvis (Wales)

Pool D

1 October, Millennium Stadium, Cardiff Arms Park

WALES.....................23 (2G 3PG)

ARGENTINA..........18 (6PG)

Wales: SP Howarth; G Thomas, M Taylor, IS Gibbs, DR James; NR Jenkins, R Howley *(captain)*; PJD Rogers, GR Jenkins, D Young, JC Quinnell, CP Wyatt, CL Charvis, LS Quinnell, BD Sinkinson

Substitution: J Jones-Hughes for Gibbs (57 mins)

Scorers: Tries: Charvis, Taylor *Conversions:* N Jenkins (2) *Penalty Goals:* N Jenkins (3)

Argentina: M Contepomi; O Bartolucci, E Simone, L Arbizu *(captain)*, DL Albanese; G Quesada, A Pichot; RD Grau, ME Ledesma, M Reggiardo, CI Fernandez Lobbe, A Allub, S Phelan, G Longo, L Ostiglia

Substitutions: R A Martin for Ostiglia (HT); OJ Hasan-Jalil for Reggiardo (50 mins); GF Camardon for Bartolucci (69 mins)

Scorer: Penalty Goals: Quesada (6)

Referee: P D O'Brien (New Zealand)

3 October, The Racecourse, Wrexham

SAMOA 43 (3G 4PG 2T)

JAPAN 9 (3PG)

Samoa: S Leaega; A So'oalo, TM Vaega, VL Tuigamala, BP Lima; SJ Bachop, S So'oalo; BP Reidy, TH Leota, R Ale, S Ta'ala, L Tone, PJ Paramore, PR Lam *(captain)*, C Glendinning

Substitutions: G E Leaupepe for Tuigamala (65 mins); O Palepoi for Tone (69 mins); S Situtu for Paramore (70 mins); MAN Mika for Reidy (77 mins); E Va'a for Bachop (80 mins); J Clarke for S So'oalo (80 mins)

Scorers: Tries: Lima (2), A So'oalo (2), Leaega *Conversions:* Leaega (3)

Penalty Goals: Leaega (4)

Japan: T Matsuda; D Ohata, A McCormick *(captain)*, Y Motoki, T Masuho; K Hirose, GTM Bachop; S Hasegawa, M Kunda, K Oguchi, R Gordon, N Okubo, Y Watanabe, JW Joseph, G Smith

Substitutions: P Tuidraki for Matsuda (28 mins); H Tanuma for Gordon (60 mins); T Ito for Okubo (65 mins); M Sakata for Kunda (71 mins); A Yoshida for Tuidraki (71 mins)

Scorer: Penalty Goals: Hirose (3)

Referee: A Cole (Australia)

WALES.....................64 (8G 1PG 1T)

JAPAN 15 (1G 1PG 1T)

Wales: SP Howarth; J Jones-Hughes, M Taylor, IS Gibbs, AG Bateman; NR Jenkins, R Howley *(captain)*; PJD Rogers, GR Jenkins, D Young, JC Quinnell, MJ Voyle, ME Williams, G Lewis, BD Sinkinson

Substitutions: G Thomas for Bateman (37 mins); ALP Lewis for Rogers (61 mins); DS Llewellyn for Howley (63 mins); JM Humphreys for G Jenkins (66 mins); S Jones for Howarth (67 mins); BR Evans for Young (73 mins); C P Wyatt for Sinkinson (79 mins)

Scorers: Tries: Taylor (2), Bateman, Howley, penalty try, Gibbs, Howarth, Llewellyn, Thomas *Conversions:* N Jenkins (8)

Penalty Goal: N Jenkins

Japan: T Hirao; D Ohata, A McCormick *(captain)*, Y Motoki, P Tuidraki; K Hirose, GTM Bachop; S Hasegawa, M Kunda, N Nakamura, R Gordon, H Tanuma, N Okubo, JW Joseph, G Smith

Substitutions: M Sakata for Kunda (HT); T Nakamichi for Hasegawa (61 mins); T Ito

Scott Quinnell (Wales)

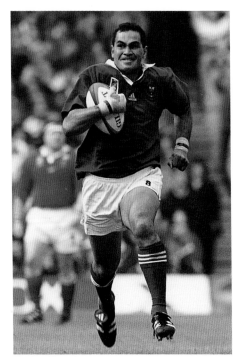

Pat Lam (Samoa)

for Okubo (67 mins); W Murata for Bachop (71 mins); Y Sakuraba for Gordon (76 mins)
Scorers: Tries: Ohata, Tuidraki
Conversion: Hirose *Penalty Goal:* Hirose
Referee: J Dumé (France)

10 October, Stradey Park, Llanelli

ARGENTINA..........**32** (8PG 1DG 1T)
SAMOA **16** (1G 3PG)
Argentina: M Contepomi; O Bartolucci, E Simone, L Arbizu *(captain)*, D L Albanese; G Quesada, A Pichot; M Reggiardo, ME Ledesma, OJ Hasan Jalil, CI Fernandez Lobbe, A Allub, S Phelan, G Longo, RA Martin
Substitutions: M A Ruiz for Longo (58 mins); GF Camardon for Bartolucci (63 mins); M Scelzo for Hasan Jalil (76 mins)
Scorers: Try: Allub *Penalty Goals:* Quesada (8)
Dropped Goal: Quesada

Samoa: S Leaega; A So'oalo, GE Leaupepe, VL Tuigamala, BP Lima; SJ Bachop, S So'oalo; BP Reidy, TH Leota, R Ale, O Palepoi, L Tone, S Ta'ala, PR Lam *(captain)*, PJ Paramore
Substitutions: K Toleafoa for Tone (52 mins); T Vili for Bachop (73 mins); MAN Mika for Reidy (77 mins); O Matauiau for Leota (80 mins); I Feaunati for Palepoi (80 mins); TM Vaega for Tuigamala (temp 64 to 65 mins)
Scorers: Try: Paramore *Conversion:* Leaega
Penalty Goals: Leaega (3)
Referee: W J Erickson (Australia)

14 October, Millennium Stadium, Cardiff Arms Park

WALES....................**31** (2G 4PG 1T)
SAMOA **38** (5G 1PG)
Wales: SP Howarth; G Thomas, M Taylor, IS Gibbs, DR James; NR Jenkins, R Howley *(captain)*; PJD Rogers, GR Jenkins, D Young, GO Llewellyn, CP Wyatt, ME Williams, LS Quinnell, BD Sinkinson
Substitutions: BR Evans for Young (54 mins); ALP Lewis for Rogers (79 mins)
Scorers: Tries: penalty tries (2), Thomas
Conversions: N Jenkins (2)
Penalty Goals: N Jenkins (4)
Samoa: S Leaega; B P Lima, T M Vaega, GE Leaupepe, VL Tuigamala; SJ Bachop, S So'oalo; BP Reidy, TH Leota, R Ale, L Falaniko, L Tone, PJ Paramore, PR Lam *(captain)*, C Glendinning
Substitutions: S Sititi for Paramore (12 mins); S Ta'ala for Falaniko (63 mins); MAN Mika for Ale (75 mins); E Va'a for Bachop (78 mins); T Fanolua for Leaupepe (78 mins); O Matauiau for Leota (78 mins)

Scorers: Tries: Bachop (2), Falaniko, Lam, Leaega *Conversions:* Leaega (5)
Penalty Goal: Leaega
Referee: E F Morrison (England)

16 October, Millennium Stadium, Cardiff Arms Park
ARGENTINA..........**33** (1G 7PG 1T)
JAPAN **12** (4PG)
Argentina: I Corleto; GF Camardon, E Simone, L Arbizu *(captain)*, DL Albanese; G Quesada, A Pichot; M Reggiardo, ME Ledesma, O J Hasan Jalil, PL Sporleder, A Allub, S Phelan, CI Fernandez Lobbe, RA Martin
Substitutions: MA Ruiz for Sporleder (53 mins); L Ostiglia for Phelan (69 mins); F Contepomi for Quesada (78 mins)
Scorers: Tries: Pichot, Albanese *Conversion:* F Contepomi *Penalty Goals:* Quesada (7)
Japan: T Matsuda; D Ohata, A McCormick *(captain)*, Y Motoki, P Tuidraki, K Hirose, GTM Bachop; T Nakamichi, M Kunda, K Oguchi, R Gordon, H Tanuma, N Okubo, JW Joseph, G Smith
Substitutions: M Sakata for Kunda (46 mins); S Hasegawa for Nakamichi (46 mins); N Nakamura for Oguchi (52 mins); T Ito for Okubo (68 mins)
Scorer: Penalty Goals: Hirose (4)
Referee: S Dickinson (Australia)

<table>
<tr><th colspan="7">POOL D FINAL TABLE</th></tr>
<tr><th></th><th>P</th><th>W</th><th>D</th><th>L</th><th>F</th><th>A</th><th>Pts</th></tr>
<tr><td>Wales</td><td>3</td><td>2</td><td>0</td><td>1</td><td>118</td><td>71</td><td>7</td></tr>
<tr><td>Samoa</td><td>3</td><td>2</td><td>0</td><td>1</td><td>97</td><td>72</td><td>7</td></tr>
<tr><td>Argentina</td><td>3</td><td>2</td><td>0</td><td>1</td><td>83</td><td>51</td><td>7</td></tr>
<tr><td>Japan</td><td>3</td><td>0</td><td>0</td><td>3</td><td>36</td><td>140</td><td>3</td></tr>
</table>

Justin Bishop (Ireland)

Pool E

2 October, Lansdowne Road, Dublin

IRELAND 53 (6G 2PG 1T)
UNITED STATES....8 (1PG 1T)

Ireland: CMP O'Shea; JP Bishop, BG O'Driscoll, KM Maggs, MR Mostyn; DG Humphreys, TA Tierney; PM Clohessy, KGM Wood, PS Wallace, PS Johns, JW Davidson, T Brennan, D O'Cuinneagain *(captain)*, AJ Ward

Substitutions: ME O'Kelly for Davidson (HT); ERP Miller for Brennan (58 mins); JM Fitzpatrick for Clohessy (58 mins); EP Elwood for Humphreys (67 mins); JC Bell for Maggs (71 mins); RP Nesdale for Wood (76 mins); B T O'Meara for Tierney (76 mins)

Scorers: Tries: Wood (4), Bishop, O'Driscoll, penalty try *Conversions:* Humphreys (4), Elwood (2) *Penalty Goals:* Humphreys (2)

United States: K Shuman; V Anitoni, J Grobler, T Takau, B Hightower; MA Williams, K Dalzell; G Sucher, TW Billups, R Lehner, L Gross, A Parker, DW Hodges, DJ Lyle *(captain)*, R Tardits

Substitutions: D Niu for Williams (48 mins); F Mo'unga for Tardits (51 mins); S Paga for Hodges (65 mins); M Scharrenberg for Takau (72 mins); K Khasigian for Billups (76 mins)

Scorer: Try: Dalzell *Penalty Goal:* Dalzell

Referee: J Dumé (France)

3 October, Ravenhill, Belfast

AUSTRALIA 57 (6G 3T)
ROMANIA.................9 (3PG)

Australia: M Burke; BN Tune, DJ Herbert, TJ Horan, JS Little; RB Kafer, GM Gregan; RLL Harry, PN Kearns, AT Blades, DT Giffin, JA Eales *(captain)*, ODA Finegan, RST Kefu, DJ Wilson

Substitutions: JWC Roff for Tune (HT); CP Strauss for Wilson (HT); JA Paul for Kearns (HT); MR Connors for Finegan (66 mins); CJ Whitaker for Gregan (66 mins); DJ Crowley for Harry (69 mins); NP Grey for Burke (80 mins)

Scorers: Tries: Kefu (3), Roff (2), Horan, Burke, Little, Paul *Conversions:* Burke (5), Eales

Romania: M Vioreanu; C Sauan, G Brezoianu, RS Gontineac *(captain)*, GL Solomie; LR Vusec, P Mitu; C Stan, PV Balan, L Rotaru, TE Brinza, O Slusariuc, AA Petrache, CS Draguceanu, E Septar

Substitutions: ND Dima for Rotaru (26 mins); D Chiriac for Slusariuc (60 mins); F Corodeanu for Draguceanu (68 mins); R Mavrodin for Stan (70 mins)

Scorer: Penalty Goals: Mitu (3)

Referee: P J Honiss (New Zealand)

9 October, Lansdowne Road, Dublin

UNITED STATES..25 (2G 2PG 1T)
ROMANIA................27 (2G 1PG 2T)

United States: K Shuman; V Anitoni, J Grobler, MA Scharrenberg, B Hightower; D Niu, K Dalzell; G Sucher, TW Billups, R Lehner, L Gross, A Parker, DJ Lyle *(captain)*, R A Lumkong, F Mo'unga

Substitutions: S Paga for Lyle (30 mins); R Tardits for Lumkong (54 mins); K Khasigian for Billups (63 mins); DW Hodges for Mo'unga (69 mins); T Takau for Scharrenberg (74 mins); J Clayton for Sucher (79 mins)

Scorers: Tries: Lyle, Hightower, Shuman *Conversions:* Dalzell (2) *Penalty Goal:* Dalzell (2)

Romania: M Vioreanu; C Sauan, G Brezoianu, RS Gontineac, GL Solomie; LR Vusec, P Mitu; R Mavrodin, PV Balan, C Stan, TE Brinza, T Constantin *(captain)*, AA Petrache, CS Draguceanu, E Septar

Substitutions: F Corodeanu for Draguceanu (temp 17 to 18 mins) and for Septar (78 mins); ND Dima for Stan (79 mins); D Chiriac for Constantin (temp 49 to 50 mins);

Scorers: Tries: Solomie (2), Constantin, Petrache *Conversions:* Mitu (2)

Penalty Goal: Mitu

Referee: J M Fleming (Scotland)

10 October, Lansdowne Road, Dublin

IRELAND 3 (1PG)

AUSTRALIA 23 (2G 3PG)

Ireland: CMP O'Shea; JP Bishop, BG O'Driscoll, KM Maggs, MR Mostyn; DG Humphreys, TA Tierney; JM Fitzpatrick, KGM Wood, PS Wallace, PS Johns, ME O'Kelly, T Brennan, D O'Cuinneagain *(captain)*, AJ Ward

Substitutions: JC Bell for Maggs (33 mins); PM Clohessy for Fitzpatrick (51 mins); ERP Miller for Brennan (temp 20 to 26 mins and 51 mins); EP Elwood for Humphreys (60 mins); R Casey for O'Kelly (temp 6 to 12 mins)

Scorer: Penalty Goal: Humphreys

Australia: M Burke; BN Tune, DJ Herbert, TJ Horan, JWC Roff; S J Larkham, GM Gregan; RLL Harry, PN Kearns, AT Blades, DT Giffin, JA Eales *(captain)*, MR Connors, RST Kefu, DJ Wilson

Substitutions: JA Paul for Kearns (9 mins); ODA Finegan for Giffin (57 mins); CP Strauss for Eales (65 mins); DJ Crowley for Paul (temp 38 mins to HT) and for

Toutai Kefu (Australia)

Harry (70 mins); NP Grey for Horan (78 mins); JS Little for Roff (temp 45 to 55 mins) and for Tune (79 mins)

Scorers: Tries: Horan, Tune *Conversions:* Burke (2) *Penalty Goals:* Burke (2), Eales

Referee: C Thomas (Wales)

14 October, Thomond Park, Limerick

AUSTRALIA 55 (6G 1PG 2T)

UNITED STATES ..19 (1G 3PG 1DG)

Australia: CE Latham; SNG Staniforth, JS Little *(captain)*, NP Grey, M Burke; SJ Larkham, CJ Whitaker; DJ Crowley, MA Foley, RS Moore, MR Connors, TM Bowman, ODA Finegan, RW Williams, CP Strauss

Substitutions: RB Kafer for Larkham (49 mins); MJ Cockbain for Williams (temp 4 to 10 mins) and for Bowman (54 mins); DT Giffin for Williams (67 mins); JWC Roff for Burke (74 mins)

Scorers: Tries: Staniforth (2), Larkham, Burke, Foley, Strauss, Whitaker, Latham *Conversions:* Burke (5), Roff *Penalty Goal:* Burke

United States: K Shuman; V Anitoni, J Grobler, MA Scharrenberg, B Hightower; D Niu, K Dalzell *(captain)*; J Clayton, TW Billups, G Sucher, L Gross, A Parker, DW Hodges, RA Lumkong, F Mo'unga

Substitutions: A Saulala for Grobler (58 mins); S Paga for Hodges (69 mins); M L'Huillier for Clayton (69 mins); K Khasigian for Billups (69 mins); T Takau for Scharrenberg (69 mins); J Coulson for Dalzell (80 mins); E Reed for Gross (80 mins)

Scorers: Try: Grobler *Conversion:* Dalzell *Penalty Goals:* Dalzell (3) *Dropped Goal:* Niu

Referee: A Watson (South Africa)

15 October, Lansdowne Road, Dublin

IRELAND 44 (5G 2PG 1DG)

ROMANIA...............14 (3PG 1T)

Ireland: CMP O'Shea; JA Topping, JC Bell, M Mullins, MR Mostyn; EP Elwood, TA Tierney; JM Fitzpatrick, RP Nesdale, PS Wallace, PS Johns, ME O'Kelly, AJ Ward, DO'Cuinneagain *(captain)*, K Dawson

Substitutions: A Quinlan for Ward (49 mins); JW Davidson for Johns (49 mins); AJW McKeen for Wallace (60 mins); BT O'Meara for Tierney (60 mins); GM D'Arcy for O'Shea (60 mins); BG O'Driscoll for Elwood (72 mins); KGM Wood for O'Cuinneagain (80 mins)

Scorers: Tries: O'Shea (2), Tierney, O'Cuinneagain, Ward *Conversions:* Elwood (5) *Penalty Goals:* Elwood (2) *Dropped Goal:* O'Driscoll

Romania: M Vioreanu; C Sauan, G Brezoianu, RS Gontineac, GL Solomie; LR Vusec, P Mitu; R Mavrodin, PV Balan, C Stan, TE Brinza, T Constantin *(captain)*, AA Petrache, CS Draguceanu, E Septar

Substitutions: F Corodeanu for Septar (46 mins); D Chiriac for Constantin (46 mins); ND Dima for Balan (60 mins); L Rotaru for Stan (63 mins); R Fugigi for Sauan (75 mins); M Jacob for Mitu (81 mins); I Tofan for Brezoianu (81 mins)

Scorers: Try: Sauan *Penalty Goals:* Mitu (3)

Referee: B Campsall (England)

POOL E FINAL TABLE							
	P	W	D	L	F	A	Pts
Australia	3	3	0	0	135	31	9
Ireland	3	2	0	1	100	45	7
Romania	3	1	0	2	50	126	5
United States	3	0	0	3	52	135	3

THE PLAY OFF MATCHES FOR QUARTER FINAL PLACES

20 October, Twickenham

ENGLAND **45** (2G 7PG 2T)

FIJI **24** (3G 1PG)

England: MB Perry; ND Beal, WJH Greenwood, MJ Catt, DD Luger; JP Wilkinson, AS Healey; J Leonard, PBT Greening, DJ Garforth, MO Johnson (*captain*), GS Archer, JPR Worsley, LBN Dallaglio, NA Back

Substitutions: GC Rowntree for Leonard (27 mins); PR de Glanville for Luger (39 mins); MJS Dawson for Healey (HT); TAK Rodber for Archer (44 mins); PJ Grayson for Wilkinson (70 mins); R Cockerill for Greening (70 mins); RA Hill for Worsley (temp HT to 78 mins) and for Perry (78 mins)

Mike Catt (England) tackled by Mosese Rauluni (Fiji)

Scorers: Tries: Greening, Luger, Back, Beal

Conversions: Wilkinson, Dawson

Penalty Goals: Wilkinson (7)

Fiji: A Uluinayau; M Vunibaka, V Satala, M Nakauta, I Tikomaimakogai; W Serevi, M Rauluni; D Rouse, G Smith (*captain*), J Veitayaki, S Raiwalui, E Katalau, K Sewabu, I Tawake, SN Tawake

Substitutions: N Little for Serevi (48 mins); I Male for I Tawake (48 mins); W Sotutu for Vunibaka (56 mins); I Rasila for Smith (73 mins); E Naituivau for Rouse (73 mins); J Rauluni for Tikomaimakogai (76 mins)

Scorers: Try: Satala, Nakauta, Tikomaimakogai

Conversions: Little (3) *Penalty Goal:* Serevi

Referee: C Thomas (Wales)

20 October, Murrayfield

SCOTLAND **35** (1G 5PG 1DG 2T)

SAMOA **20** (2G 2PG)

Scotland: GH Metcalfe; CA Murray, MJM Mayer, JG McLaren, KM Logan; GPJ Townsend, G Armstrong (*captain*); TJ Smith, GC Bulloch, G Graham, S Murray, GW Weir, MD Leslie, GL Simpson, AC Pountney

Substitutions: CG Mather for Pountney (58 mins); SB Grimes for S Murray (70 mins); DW Hodge for Townsend (74 mins); AP Burnell for Graham (78 mins); RR Russell for M Leslie (80 mins)

Scorers: Tries: M Leslie, penalty try, C Murray

Conversion: Logan *Penalty Goals:* Logan (5)

Dropped Goal: Townsend

Samoa: S Leaega; BP Lima, TM Vaega, T Fanolua, VL Tuigamala; SJ Bachop, S So'oalo; BP Reidy, TH Leota, S Asi, L Falaniko, L Tone, S Sititi, PR Lam (*captain*), C Glendinning

Substitutions: O Matauiau for Leota (36 mins); S Ta'ala for Falaniko (58 mins); R Ale for Asi (65 mins); E Va'a for Bachop (71 mins); F Toala for Vaega (75 mins)

Scorers: Tries: Sititi, Lima *Conversions:* Leaega (2) *Penalty Goals:* Leaega (2)

Referee: DTM McHugh (Ireland)

20 October, Stade Felix Bollaert, Lens

IRELAND **24** (7PG 1DG)

ARGENTINA **28** (1G 7PG)

Ireland: CMP O'Shea; JP Bishop, BG O'Driscoll, KM Maggs, MR Mostyn; DG Humphreys, TA Tierney; R Corrigan, KGM Wood, PS Wallace, JW Davidson, ME O'Kelly, AJ Ward, D O'Cuinneagain (*captain*), K Dawson

Substitutions: R Casey for Davidson (60 mins); JM Fitzpatrick for Wallace (temp 64 to 71 mins) and for Corrigan (71 mins); ERP Miller for Ward (77 mins)

Scorer: Penalty Goals: Humphreys (7)

Dropped Goal: Humphreys

Argentina: I Corleto; GF Camardon, E Simone, L Arbizu (*captain*), DL Albanese; G Quesada, A Pichot; M Reggiardo, ME Ledesma, OJ Hasan Jalil, CI Fernandez Lobbe, A Allub, S Phelan, G Longo, RA Martin

Substitutions: M Scelzo for Hasan Jalil (51 mins); F Contepomi for Corleto (68 mins)

Scorers: Try: Albanese *Conversion:* Quesada

Penalty Goals: Quesada (7)

Referee: S Dickinson (Australia)

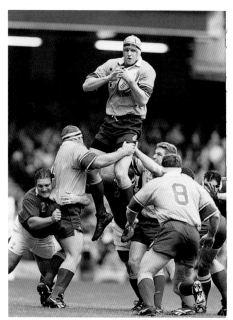

David Giffin (Australia)

THE QUARTER FINALS

23 October, Millennium Stadium, Cardiff Arms Park

WALES 9 (3PG)

AUSTRALIA 24 (3G 1PG)

Wales: SP Howarth; G Thomas, M Taylor, IS Gibbs, DR James; NR Jenkins, R Howley *(captain)*; PJD Rogers, GR Jenkins, D Young, JC Quinnell, CP Wyatt, CL Charvis, LS Quinnell, BD Sinkinson

Substitutions: BR Evans for Young (38 mins); AG Bateman for Thomas (52 mins); MJ Voyle for C Quinnell (71 mins); ALP Lewis for Rogers (71 mins)

Scorer: Penalty Goals: N Jenkins (3)

Australia: M Burke; BN Tune, DJ Herbert, TJ Horan, JWC Roff; SJ Larkham, GM Gregan; RLL Harry, MA Foley, AT Blades, DT Giffin, JA Eales *(captain)*, M J Cockbain, CP Strauss, DJ Wilson

Substitutions: ODA Finegan for Cockbain (61

mins); JS Little for Tune (78 mins); MR Connors for Eales (85 mins); JA Paul for Foley (temp 71 to 73 mins)

Scorers: Tries: Gregan (2), Tune *Conversions:* Burke (3) *Penalty Goal:* Burke

Referee: C J Hawke (New Zealand)

24 October, Stade de France, Paris

SOUTH AFRICA ..44 (2G 5PG 5DG)

ENGLAND 21 (7PG)

South Africa: PC Montgomery; DJ Kayser, RF Fleck, PG Muller, PWG Rossouw; JH de Beer, JH van der Westhuizen *(captain)*; JP du Randt, AE Drotské, IJ Visagie, K Otto, MG Andrews, JC Erasmus, RB Skinstad, AG Venter

Substitutions: A-H le Roux for du Randt (62 mins); PA van den Berg for Andrews (67 mins); AN Vos for Skinstad (76 mins); CS Terblanche for Kayser (63 to 66 mins)

Scorers: Tries: Rossouw, van der Westhuizen *Conversions:* de Beer (2) *Penalty Goals:* de Beer (5) *Dropped Goals:* de Beer (5)

England: MB Perry; ND Beal, WJH Greenwood, PR de Glanville, DD Luger; PJ Grayson, MJS Dawson; J Leonard, PBT Greening, PJ Vickery, MO Johnson *(captain)*, DJ Grewcock, RA Hill, LBN Dallaglio, NA Back

Substitutions: AS Healey for Beal (55 mins); JP Wilkinson for Grayson (55 mins); MJ Catt for de Glanville (71 mins); ME Corry for Dawson (72 mins)

Scorers: Penalty Goals: Grayson (6), Wilkinson

Referee: J M Fleming (Scotland)

24 October, Lansdowne Road, Dublin

FRANCE 47 (5G 4PG)

ARGENTINA 26 (2G 4PG)

France: X Garbajosa; P Bernat-Salles, R Dourthe, E Ntamack, C Dominici; C Lamaison, F Galthié; C Soulette, R Ibañez *(captain)*, F Tournaire, A Benazzi, O Brouzet, M Lièvremont, C Juillet, O Magne

Substitutions: P de Villiers for Soulette (59 mins); A Costes for Juillet (65 mins); S Castaignède for Galthié (70 mins); M Dal Maso for Ibañez (77 mins); D Auradou for Benazzi (79 mins); U Mola for Garbajosa (81 mins); S Glas for Dourthe (81 mins)

Scorers: Tries: Garbajosa (2), Bernat-Salles (2), Ntamack *Conversions:* Lamaison (5) *Penalty Goals:* Lamaison (4)

Jannie de Beer and Joost van der Westhuizen (South Africa)

Cameron Murray (Scotland)

Argentina: I Corleto; GF Camardon, E Simone, L Arbizu *(captain)*, DL Albanese; G Quesada, A Pichot; RD Grau, ME Ledesma, M Reggiardo, CI Fernandez Lobbe, A Allub, S Phelan, G Longo, RA Martin

Substitutions: MA Ruiz for Fernandez Lobbe (31 mins); M Scelzo for Reggiardo (48 mins); F Contepomi for Quesada (60 mins); L Ostiglia for Phelan (temp 44 to 47 mins and from 62 mins); M Contepomi for Albanese (temp 44 to 47 mins) and for Simone (75 mins); N Fernandez Miranda for Pichot (81 mins); A Canalda for Ledesma (81 mins)

Scorers: Try: Pichot, Arbizu *Conversions:* Quesada (2) *Penalty Goals:* Quesada (3), F Contepomi

Referee: W D Bevan (Wales)

24 October, Murrayfield

SCOTLAND 18 (1G 1PG 1DG 1T)

NEW ZEALAND ..30 (2G 2PG 2T)

Scotland: GH Metcalfe; CA Murray, AV Tait, MJM Mayer, KM Logan; GPJ Townsend, G Armstrong *(captain)*; TJ Smith, GC Bulloch, AP Burnell, S Murray, GW Weir, MD Leslie, GL Simpson, AC Pountney

Substitutions: SB Grimes for Weir (54 mins); G Graham for Burnell (54 mins); RR Russell for Bulloch (68 mins)

Scorers: Tries: Pountney, C Murray *Conversion:* Logan *Penalty Goal:* Logan *Dropped Goal:* Townsend

New Zealand: JW Wilson; TJF Umaga, CM Cullen, A Ieremia, JT Lomu; AP Mehrtens, JW Marshall; CH Hoeft, AD Oliver, CW Dowd, NM Maxwell, RM Brooke, RD Thorne, TC Randell *(captain)*, JA Kronfeld

Substitutions: TE Brown for Mehrtens (HT); MG Hammett for Oliver (60 mins); ID Jones for Maxwell (62 mins); KJ Meeuws for Hoeft (74 mins); DPE Gibson for Umaga (76 mins)

Scorers: Tries: Umaga (2), Wilson, Lomu *Conversions:* Mehrtens (2) *Penalty Goals:* Mehrtens (2)

Referee: E F Morrison (England)

THE SEMI FINALS

30 October, Twickenham

SOUTH AFRICA....21 (6PG 1DG)

AUSTRALIA ....27 (8PG 1DG)(aet)

South Africa: PC Montgomery; DJ Kayser, RF Fleck, PG Muller, PWG Rossouw; JH de Beer, JH van der Westhuizen *(captain)*; JP du Randt, AE Drotské, IJ Visagie, K Otto, MG Andrews, JC Erasmus, RB Skinstad, AG Venter

Substitutions: A-H le Roux for du Randt (59 mins); PA van den Berg for Andrews (59 mins); AN Vos for Skinstad (temp 71 to 82 mins and from 84 mins); CS Terblanche for Kayser (72 mins); HW Honiball for Muller (ET)

Scorer: Penalty Goals: de Beer (6)

Dropped Goal: de Beer

Australia: M Burke; BN Tune, DJ Herbert, TJ Horan, JWC Roff; SJ Larkham, GM Gregan; RLL Harry, MA Foley, AT Blades, DT Giffin, JA Eales *(captain)*, MJ Cockbain, RST Kefu, DJ Wilson

Substitutions: ODA Finegan for Cockbain (58 mins); JS Little for Tune (temp 61 to 99 mins) and for Herbert (99 mins); NP Grey for Horan (74 mins); MR Connors for Giffin (92 mins)

Scorers: Penalty Goals: Burke (8)

Dropped Goal: Larkham

Referee: W D Bevan (Wales)

---

31 October, Twickenham

NEW ZEALAND 31 (2G 4PG 1T)

FRANCE 43 (4G 3PG 2DG)

New Zealand: JW Wilson; TJF Umaga, CM Cullen, A Ieremia, JT Lomu; AP Mehrtens, BT Kelleher; CH Hoeft, AD Oliver, CW Dowd, NM Maxwell, RM Brooke, RD Thorne, TC Randell *(captain)*, JA Kronfeld

Substitutions: KJ Meeuws for Dowd (57 mins); DPE Gibson for Ieremia (57 mins); RK Willis for Brooke (71 mins); JW Marshall for Kelleher (78 mins)

Scorers: Tries: Lomu (2), Wilson *Conversions:* Mehrtens (2) *Penalty Goals:* Mehrtens (4)

France: X Garbajosa; P Bernat-Salles, R Dourthe, E Ntamack, C Dominici; C Lamaison, F Galthié; C Soulette, R Ibañez *(captain)*, F Tournaire, A Benazzi, F Pelous, M Lièvremont, C Juillet, O Magne

Substitutions: O Brouzet for Juillet (31 mins); P de Villiers for Soulette (57 mins); A Costes for Lièvremont (64 mins); S Castaignède for Galthié (75 mins); U Mola for Dominici (77 mins); S Glas for Ntamack (80 mins)

Scorers: Tries: Lamaison, Dominici, Dourthe, Bernat-Salles *Conversions:* Lamaison (4) *Penalty Goals:* Lamaison (3) *Dropped Goals:* Lamaison (2)

Referee: J M Fleming (Scotland)

THE THIRD/FOURTH PLACE PLAY-OFF

4 November, Millennium Stadium, Cardiff Arms Park

SOUTH AFRICA....22 (1G 3PG 2DG)

NEW ZEALAND 18 (6PG)

South Africa: PC Montgomery; BJ Paulse, RF Fleck, PG Muller, CS Terblanche; HW Honiball, JH van der Westhuizen *(captain)*; JP du Randt, AE Drotské, IJ Visagie, K Otto, MG Andrews, JC Erasmus, AN Vos, AG Venter

Substitutions: A-H le Roux for du Randt (49 mins); PA van den Berg for Andrews (66 mins); RJ Kruger for Vos (74 mins); CLC Rossouw for Drotské (76 mins); W Swanepoel for van der Westhuizen (temp 59 to 66 mins)

Scorers: Try: Paulse *Conversion:* Honiball

Penalty Goals: Honiball (3) *Dropped Goals:* Montgomery (2)

New Zealand: JW Wilson; TJF Umaga, CM Cullen, A Ieremia, JT Lomu; AP Mehrtens, JW Marshall; CW Dowd, MG Hammett, KJ Meeuws, NM Maxwell, RK Willis, RD Thorne, TC Randell *(captain)*, JA Kronfeld

Substitutions: PF Alatini for Umaga (HT); CH Hoeft for Dowd (51 mins); DG Mika for Thorne (66 mins); AD Oliver for Hammett (71 mins)

Scorer: Penalty Goals: Mehrtens (6)

Referee: P Marshall (Australia)

THE FINAL

6 November, Millennium Stadium, Cardiff Arms Park

AUSTRALIA **35** (2G 7PG)

FRANCE **12** (4PG)

Australia: M Burke; BN Tune, DJ Herbert, TJ Horan, JWC Roff; SJ Larkham, GM Gregan; RLL Harry, MA Foley, AT Blades, DT Giffin, JA Eales *(captain)*, MJ Cockbain, RST Kefu, DJ Wilson

Substitutions: JS Little for Herbert (46 mins); ODA Finegan for Cockbain (52 mins); MR Connors for Wilson (73 mins); DJ Crowley for Harry (75 mins); JA Paul for Foley (85 mins); CJ Whitaker for Gregan (86 mins); NP Grey for Horan (86 mins)

Scorers: Tries: Tune, Finegan

Conversions: Burke (2) *Penalty Goals:* Burke (7)

France: X Garbajosa; P Bernat-Salles, R Dourthe, E Ntamack, C Dominici; C Lamaison, F Galthié; C Soulette, R Ibañez *(captain)*, F Tournaire, A Benazzi, F Pelous, M Lièvremont, C Juillet, O Magne

Substitutions: O Brouzet for Juillet (HT); P de Villiers for Soulette (47 mins); A Costes for Magne (temp 19 to 22 mins) and for Lièvremont (67 mins); U Mola for Garbajosa (67 mins); S Glas for Dourthe (temp 49 to 55 mins and from 74 mins); S Castaignède for Galthié (76 mins); M Dal Maso for Ibañez (79 mins)

Scorer: Penalty Goals: Lamaison (4)

Referee: A Watson (South Africa)

RUGBY WORLD CUP 1999
LEADING SCORING RECORDS

Most points by a team in match:

101	New Zealand v Italy	101-3
101	England v Tonga	101-10
72	Canada v Namibia	72-11
67	England v Italy	67-7
67	Fiji v Namibia	67-18
64	Wales v Japan	64-15

Most tries by a team in a match

14	New Zealand v Italy
13	England v Tonga
9	Wales v Japan
9	Canada v Namibia
9	Australia v Romania
9	Fiji v Namibia

Most points by a player in a match

36	Paul Grayson	England v Tonga
36	Tony Brown	New Zealand v Italy
34	Jannie de Beer	South Africa v England
32	Jonny Wilkinson	England v Italy
28	Christophe Lamaison	France v New Zealand
27	Gareth Rees	Canada v Namibia
27	Gonzalo Quesada	Argentina v Samoa

Grayson's 36 points was a new England Test record and de Beer's 34 a new South Africa Test record. De Beer's 34 included five dropped goals, a new world record for a major Test.

Most tries by a player in a match

4	Keith Wood	Ireland v United States
3	Toutai Kefu	Australia v Romania
3	Ugo Mola	France v Namibia
3	Jeff Wilson	New Zealand v Italy

Keith Wood became the first hooker to score four tries in a major international. In doing so, he equalled the Ireland record for most tries in a Test.

Players scoring with a full house of actions

Sateki Tu'ipulotu	Tonga v Italy
Christophe Lamaison	France v New Zealand

Lamaison performed the feat for the second time in Twickenham Tests. He had scored a full set when leading a remarkable French comeback against England at Twickenham in 1997.

Leading overall points scorers in the competition

102	Gonzalo Quesada	Argentina
101	Matthew Burke	Australia
97	Jannie de Beer	South Africa
79	Andrew Mehrtens	New Zealand
69	Jonny Wilkinson	England
65	Christophe Lamaison	France
62	Silao Leaega	Samoa
57	Neil Jenkins	Wales
54	Paul Grayson	England
51	Kenny Logan	Scotland

Quesada's haul included 31 penalty goals and de Beer's six dropped goals, both new records for the final stages of a Rugby World Cup tournament. Jenkins took his total in Tests for Wales and the Lions past the previous world record of 911 points established by Australia's Michael Lynagh.

Leading overall try scorers in the competition

8	Jonah Lomu	New Zealand
6	Jeff Wilson	New Zealand
4	Keith Wood	Ireland
4	Dan Luger	England
4	Viliami Satala	Fiji
4	Philippe Bernat-Salles	France

Lomu's eight tries set a new record for most scored in one tournament. He has now scored 15 tries altogether in World Cup final stages, a new overall record.

Jonah Lomu (New Zealand)

OLDEST, YOUNGEST, TALLEST, SHORTEST, HEAVIEST, AND LIGHTEST IN RUGBY WORLD CUP 1999

Diego Ormaechea (Uruguay)

The Oldest

Name	Nation	Position	Born	Age on 1.10.99
Diego Ormaechea	Uruguay	No 8	19.07.59	40yrs 2mths 12 days
Mark Cardinal	Canada	Hooker	05.05.61	38yrs 4mths 26 days
Mark Williams	USA	Utility back	26.06.61	38yrs 3mths 5 days
Ifereimi Tawake	Fiji	Flanker/Lock	21.07.62	37yrs 2mths 10 days
Julian Loveday	Canada	Utility back	26.03.63	36yrs 6mths 5 days
Jose Diaz	Spain	Flanker	31.03.63	36yrs 6mths 1 day
Rich Schurfeld	USA	Wing	19.04.63	36yrs 5mths 12 days
Francisco Puertas	Spain	Full-back	18.11.63	35yrs 10mths 13 days
Kuli Faletau	Tonga	Lock	30.12.63	35yrs 9mths 2days
Alberto Malo	Spain	Flanker	03.04.64	35yrs 5mths 28 days

The Youngest

Name	Nation	Position	Born	Age on 1.10.99
Ovidiu Tonita	Romania	Lock	06.08.80	19 yrs 1 mth 25 days
Gordon D'Arcy	Ireland	Full-back	10.02.80	19 yrs 7 mths 21 days
Nicolae Dima	Romania	Hooker	30.07.79	20 yrs 2 mths 2 days
Sinapati Uiagalelei	USA	Wing	21.06.79	20 yrs 3 mths 10 days
Jonny Wilkinson	England	Outside-half	25.05.79	20 yrs 4 mths 6 days
Hannes Theron	Namibia	Lock	07.05.79	20 yrs 4 mths 24 days
Mauro Bergamasco	Italy	Wing/Flanker	01.05.79	20 yrs 4 mths 30 days
Martin Cervino	Uruguay	Full-back	22.04.79	20 yrs 5 mths 9 days
'Epeli Taione	Tonga	Wing/Flanker	02.03.79	20 yrs 6 mths 29 days
Brian O'Driscoll	Ireland	Centre	21.01.79	20 yrs 8 mths 10 days

The Tallest

Name	Nation	Position	Metric	Imperial
Luke Gross	USA	Lock	206 cm	6' 9"
Eric Reed	USA	Lock	203 cm	6' 8"
Olivier Brouzet	France	Lock	203 cm	6' 8"
John Tait	Canada	Lock	203 cm	6' 8"
David Auradou	France	Lock	202 cm	6' 7_"
Robert Casey	Ireland	Lock	201 cm	6' 7"
Malcolm O'Kelly	Ireland	Lock	201 cm	6' 7"
Albert van den Berg	South Africa	Lock	201 cm	6' 7"
Doddie Weir	Scotland	Lock	201 cm	6' 7"
Tom Bowman	Australia	Lock	201 cm	6' 7"

Imperial measures given to nearest half-inch

The Shortest

Name	Nation	Position	Metric	Imperial
Riaan Jantjies	Namibia	Scrum-half	154 cm	5' 0"
Ronaldo Pedro	Namibia	Scrum-half	167 cm	5' 5"
Keiji Hirose	Japan	Outside-half	168 cm	5' 6"
Fernando Sosa Diaz	Uruguay	Scrum-half	168 cm	5' 6"
Pierre Mignoni	France	Scrum-half	169 cm	5' 6"
Stéphane Castaignède	France	Scrum-half	170 cm	5' 7"
Alfred Uluinayau	Fiji	Centre	170 cm	5' 7"
Bryan Redpath	Scotland	Scrum-half	170 cm	5' 7"
George Graham	Scotland	Prop	170 cm	5' 7"
Tanner Vili	Samoa	Utility back	170 cm	5' 7"
Earl Va'a	Samoa	Outside-half	170 cm	5' 7"

Imperial measures given to nearest half-inch

The Heaviest

Name	Nation	Position	Metric	Imperial
Joeli Veitayaki	Fiji	Prop	130 kg	20st 6lb
Os du Randt	South Africa	Prop	130 kg	20st 6lb
Pablo Lemoine	Uruguay	Prop	130 kg	20st 6lb
Craig Quinnell	Wales	Lock	130 kg	20st 6lb
Martin Scelzo	Argentina	Prop	130 kg	20st 6lb

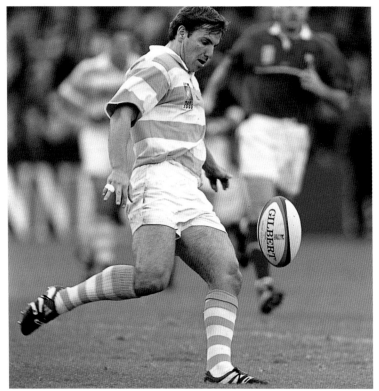
Gonzalo Quesada (Argentina)

Phil Vickery	England	Prop	126 kg	19st 12lb
Fifita Puku Faletau	Tonga	Prop	123 kg	19st 5lb
Robert Casey	Ireland	Lock	123 kg	19st 5lb
Adrian Salageanu	Romania	Prop	122 kg	19st 3lb
Ollie le Roux	South Africa	Prop	122 kg	19st 3lb

Imperial measures given to nearest pound

The Ten Lightest

Name	Nation	Position	Metric	Imperial
Riaan Jantjies	Namibia	Scrum-half	66 kg	10 st 5 lb
Stéphane Castaignède	France	Scrum-half	70 kg	11 st 0 lb
Alfonso Cardoso	Uruguay	Full-back	70 kg	11 st 0 lb
Aratz Gallastegui	Spain	Scrum-half	71 kg	11 st 2 lb
Pierre Mignoni	France	Scrum-half	71 kg	11 st 2 lb
Oriol Ripol	Spain	Wing	73 kg	11 st 7 lb
Keiji Hirose	Japan	Outside-half	73 kg	11 st 7 lb
Waturu Murata	Japan	Scrum-half	74 kg	11 st 9 lb
Ronaldo Pedro	Namibia	Scrum-half	75 kg	11 st 11 lb
Glovin van Wyk	Namibia	Full-back	75 kg	11 st 11 lb
Jaime Alonso	Spain	Scrum-half	75 kg	11 st 11 lb
Tanner Vili	Samoa	Utility back	75 kg	11 st 11 lb
Ionut Tofan	Romania	Outside-half	75 kg	11 st 11 lb

Imperial measures given to nearest pound

OVERALL COMPETITION RECORDS

First Four Rugby World Cups (Final stages only)

OVERALL RECORDS

Most overall points in final stages

227	A G Hastings	Scotland	1987-95
195	M P Lynagh	Australia	1987-95
170	G J Fox	New Zealand	1987-91

Most overall tries in final stages

15	J T Lomu	New Zealand	1995-99
11	R Underwood	England	1987-95
10	D I Campese	Australia	1987-95

LEADING SCORERS

Most points in one competition

126	G J Fox	New Zealand	1987
112	T Lacroix	France	1995
104	A G Hastings	Scotland	1995
102	G Quesada	Argentina	1999
101	M Burke	Australia	1999

Most tries in one competition

8	J T Lomu	New Zealand	1999
7	M C G Ellis	New Zealand	1995
7	J T Lomu	New Zealand	1995

Most conversions in one competition

30	G J Fox	New Zealand	1987
20	S D Culhane	New Zealand	1995
20	M P Lynagh	Australia	1987

Most penalty goals in one competition

31	G Quesada	Argentina	1999
26	T Lacroix	France	1995
21	G J Fox	New Zealand	1987
20	C R Andrew	England	1995

Most dropped goals in one competition

6	J H de Beer	South Africa	1999
3	G P J Townsend	Scotland	1999
3	A P Mehrtens	New Zealand	1995
3	J T Stransky	South Africa	1995
3	C R Andrew	England	1995
3	J Davies	Wales	1987

MOST POINTS IN A MATCH

By a team

145	New Zealand v Japan	1995
101	New Zealand v Italy	1999
101	England v Tonga	1999

89 ....Scotland v Ivory Coast 1995
74 ....New Zealand v Fiji 1987
72 ....Canada v Namibia 1999

By a player

45 ....S D Culhane................New Zealand v Japan........1995
44 ....A G Hastings ....Scotland v Ivory Coast......1995
36 ....T E Brown ....New Zealand v Italy 1999
36 ....P J Grayson................England v Tonga..............1999
34 ....J H de Beer ....South Africa v England 1999
32 .....J P Wilkinson ....England v Italy.................1999

MOST TRIES IN A MATCH

By a team

21 ....New Zealand v Japan 1995
14 ....New Zealand v Italy...............1999
13 ....England v Tonga.....................1999
13 ....Scotland v Ivory Coast 1995
13 ....France v Zimbabwe 1987

By a player

6 ....M C G Ellis ......New Zealand v Japan.................1995
4 ....K G M Wood ....Ireland v United States 1999
4 ....A G Hastings ....Scotland v Ivory Coast 1995
4 ....C M Williams .....South Africa v Western Samoa ..1995
4 ....J T Lomu ....New Zealand v England 1995
4 ....B F Robinson ....Ireland v Zimbabwe 1991
4 ....I C Evans ....Wales v Canada........................1987
4 ....C I Green ....New Zealand v Fiji.....................1987
4 ....J A Gallagher ...New Zealand v Fiji.....................1987

MOST CONVERSIONS IN A MATCH

By a team

20 ....New Zealand v Japan 1995
12 ....England v Tonga.....................1999
11 ....New Zealand v Italy...............1999
10 ....New Zealand v Fiji 1987
9 ....Canada v Namibia 1999
9 ....Scotland v Ivory Coast 1995
9 ....France v Zimbabwe 1987

By a player

20 ....S D Culhane......New Zealand v Japan.................1995
12 ....P J Grayson........England v Tonga.......................1999
11 ....T E Brown ....New Zealand v Italy 1999
10 ....G J Fox ....New Zealand v Fiji....................1987
9 ....G L Rees ....Canada v Namibia 1999
9 ....A G Hastings ....Scotland v Ivory Coast 1995
9 ....D Camberabero France v Zimbabwe 1987

Matt Burke (Australia)

MOST PENALTY GOALS IN A MATCH

By a team

8 ....Australia v South Africa 1999
8 ....Argentina v Samoa 1999
8 ....Scotland v Tonga 1995
8 ....France v Ireland 1995

By a player

8 ....M Burke ....Australia v South Africa 1999
8 ....G Quesada ....Argentina v Samoa 1999
8 ....A G Hastings ....Scotland v Tonga 1995
8 ....T Lacroix ....France v Ireland 1995

MOST DROPPED GOALS IN A MATCH

By a team

5 ....South Africa v England 1999
3 ....Fiji v Romania 1991

By a player

5 ....J H de Beer ......South Africa v England 1999
2 ....P C Montgomery South Africa v New Zealand 1999
2 ....J T Stransky ......South Africa v New Zealand 1995
2 ....C R Andrew ......England v Argentina 1995
2 ....T Rabaka ....Fiji v Romania 1991
2 ....L Arbizu ....Argentina v Australia 1991
2 ....J Davies ....Wales v Ireland.....................1987

Rugby World Cup 1999

Winners: Australia

Finalist: France

3rd Place:
South Africa

Semi-Finalist:
New Zealand